P9-ELR-907

M

Communication Research
and Broadcasting No. 2

Editors:
Internationales Zentralinstitut
für das Jugend- und Bildungsfernsehen (IZI),

Hertha Sturm

Effects and Functions of Television: Children and Adolescents

A bibliography of selected
research literature 1970–1978

Compiled by
Manfred Meyer and Ursula Nissen

K·G·Saur
München · New York · London · Paris 1981
Linnet Books · Hamden, Connecticut

LB
1044.7
M49

7464531   12/30/81 by

Editor of the series:
Professor Dr. Hertha Sturm, University of Munich, Scientific Director of the IZI

Editorial staff:
Rosemarie Hagemeister, Käthe Nowacek, Christina Undritz

IZI Documentation Department:
Paul Löhr (responsible), Manfred Meyer

Address of editor and editorial office:
Internationales Zentralinstitut für das Jugend- und Bildungsfernsehen, Rundfunkplatz 1, D-8000 München 2
Telephone (0 89) 59 00–21 40, Telex 05 29831

This publication is the revised English edition of the Bibliographical Information Service No. 1, published by the IZI in 1977

K. G. Saur Verlag KG
Pössenbacherstr. 2 b, POB 711009
D-8000 München 71
Federal Republic of Germany
Tel. (089) 79 89 01
Telex 5212067 saur d

Linnet Books
an imprint of
The Shoe String Press, Inc.
P. O. Box 4327
995 Sherman Avenue
Hamden, Connecticut 06514
Tel. (203) 248-6307

CIP-Kurztitelaufnahme der Deutschen Bibliothek

Meyer, Manfred
Effects and functions of television, children
and adolescents : a bibliogr. of selected research
literature 1970–1978 / comp. by Manfred Meyer
and Ursula Nissen. – Rev. English ed. – München,
New York, London, Paris : Saur, 1979.
  (Communication research and broadcasting ; No. 2)
  Ausg. beim Internat. Zentralinst. für d. Jugend-
u. Bildungsfernsehen, München, u.d.T.: Meyer,
Manfred: Wirkungen und Funktionen des Fern-
sehens, Kinder und Jugendliche.
  ISBN 3-598-20201-6 (München)

NE: Nissen, Ursula:

Library of Congress Cataloging in Publication Data

Meyer, Manfred .
  Effects and functions of television – children
and adolescents.

  Rev. translation of: Wirkungen und Funktionen
des Fernsehens, Kinder und Jugendliche.
  Reprint. Originally published: Rev. English
ed. München ; New York : K. G. Saur, 1979.
(Communication research and broadcasting ; no. 2)
  Includes index.
  1. Television in education – Research – Bibliog-
raphy. I. Nissen, Ursula. II. Title.
III. Series: Communication research and broad-
casting ; no. 2.
Z5814.T45M4913   1981   [LB1044.7]   302.2s   81-6000
ISBN 0-208-01924-3 (pbk.)   [016.3052'3]   AACR2

©1981 by K. G. Saur Verlag KG, München
Reprinted by K. G. Saur and in the U.S.A.
by Linnet Books
an imprint of
The Shoe String Press, Inc.
Printed and bound
by Hain Druck GmbH, Meisenheim/Glan

Editorial

The service which we attempt to provide by publishing this bibliography is to be seen in connection with the changed functions of the Internationales Zentralinstitut für das Jugend- und Bildungsfernsehen (IZI). In the course of a reorganization, a new departmental area has been added to the IZI, namely "Research and Research Observation", with particular emphasis on psychological research on media effects. Hence, our own research activities as well as the observation of research at home and abroad focus on the recipient and his multivarious dependencies. The boundlessness of which media research is occasionally accused, and the fact that there is as yet no clearly outlined communication and media theory, account in part for this self-restriction in our work. One is therefore well advised if one proceeds along the lines of the methods, approaches, and findings which other fields of scientific/empirical research have provided and which are relevant to communication and media research as well. After all, it is a question of incorporating, further developing and re-stating the criteria of psychology and social science into new areas of activity and thus into the overall work of the IZI.

This brings us to the IZI's second field of activity, "Publicity" which, to be precise, involves putting research findings into media practice. As a department of a broadcasting organization, the IZI has to concern itself with the problems and needs of the media practitioner as well. We are called upon to establish a workable relationship between media research and media practice. This is being done through seminars, through counselling activities of various kinds, through regular publications, especially through our periodical "Fernsehen und Bildung", sub-titled "International Review for Media Psychology and Media Practice".

It is quite obvious that the activities mentioned so far can only be tackled in a proper manner if there is a departmental area "behind the scenes" which does the donkey-work of collecting, sorting out and evaluating research reports and theoretical approaches. This is the "Documentation" area which in turn is based upon an efficient specialized library. Supplying information to the areas "Research and Research Observation" and "Publicity", the "Documentation" area has material at its disposal which can be allocated to certain questions and thus provides a first introduction into fields of publications and problems which still need to be prepared and structured.

459621

ALUMNI MEMORIAL LIBRARY
Creighton University
Omaha, Nebraska 68178

We are well aware of the transitory and incomplete character of this kind of work. Since we intend to compile further subject bibliographies, I would welcome specific supplementations and suggestions from my colleagues in various parts of the world.

Professor Dr. Hertha Sturm
Scientific Director of the IZI

Contents

Notes on the use of the bibliography

This is the second, revised and enlarged edition of a bibliography of selected research literature which was originally published in German in 1977.

The references listed here deal with the behaviour of young recipients in the process of mass communication. In keeping with the scope of activities and the main points of emphasis in the work of the IZI, this bibliography concentrates on the use of television and its varying functions for children and adolescents, and above all, on the effects of television programmes on their personality development and socialization.

The bibliographical data were selected according to the following criteria:

1. In general, empirical studies, research reviews and summarizing literature on special fields of research have been included only if they are based on empirical research findings. Consequently, we did not consider predominantly theoretical and methodological treatises, critical or polemical essays, conference reports or popular literature since they do not or only insufficiently substantiate research results with evidence — although they may occasionally refer to research findings.

2. In accordance with the restriction mentioned above, works on content analysis as well as studies on the behaviour and concepts of communicators, educators or government officials were also excluded. There are, however, numerous references to these areas of research in the bibliographies listed in the first chapter.

3. The selection was restricted to studies published from 1970 to about March 1978. As to research works that appeared before 1970, we refer to earlier compilations, particularly those of Atkins, Murray and Nayman (1971; see No. 24), which contains 496 entries, 285 of them with abstracts, and of Comstock et al. (1975; see Nos. 6—8), which provides more than 2300 citations and appr. 400 detailed abstracts of the so-called "key studies".

4. This bibliography contains only references to publications in English, French and German. French and German titles have been translated into English and are given in brackets after the original title. Some information on the state of research in other language areas may be found in the third chapter in the form of reports which provide a general review. In this respect we refer to the reports published in the special English issue of the IZI's periodical "Fernsehen und Bildung", vol. 9, No. 2/3 (see No. 112), which is still available. Moreover, the IZI will be pleased to provide information on other sources such as national or regional centres of documentation and research.

5. Another criterion for selection was the availability or accessibility of pertinent literature. As a rule, the compilers had the original documents at their disposal. It was possible to obtain most of the titles through the book-trade or — especially in the case of publications in specialized journals — through the public lending libraries run by the state, through university libraries or by the America Houses in the Federal Republic of Germany. Literature not available through these channels was excluded.

6. In general, it was considered superfluous to include references to almost inaccessible literature, i. e. unpublished manuscripts and dissertations, conference papers, working papers and the like. In several cases, however, references to important research projects were accepted even if they have not, or have not yet been published but are nevertheless available as "ERIC documents". This was done particularly in cases in which according to the authors research reports are obtainable only through the ERIC Reproduction Service. Whenever possible, we mentioned — in brackets in the last line of an entry — the accession number to these documents (Arlington, Va.: ERIC ED . . .). They can be ordered in the form of either hard copies or (very much cheaper) microfiches from:

> ERIC Documents Reproduction Service
> P.O. Box 190, Arlington, Virginia 22210, USA

There are, however, numerous institutions in all parts of the world that store ERIC material and offer reproduction services. They are listed in the 'Directory of ERIC Microfiche Collections', published by the National Institute of Education, Washington, D.C. It is available from:

> ERIC Processing and Reference Facility
> 4833 Rugby Avenue
> Suite 303
> Bethesda, Maryland 20014

We were guided by pragmatic considerations in dividing up the contents of the bibliography. The traditional rules of documentation would have prevented us from making detailed sub-divisions and would have required us to produce a systematically built up set of descriptors in order to make the individual phenomena accessible. But so far, there is no reliable system of descriptors by which the complicated subject of media and communication research could be defined. Such a system is being worked out by the IZI at present. Anyone who is familiar with methods of documentation knows the time and problems involved in developing such a system of annotations. It was firstly a matter of filling some of the gaps in the international exchange of research information as quickly as possible; and secondly, of enabling the user to recognize the most important directions and subject areas with which the social sciences are concerned as regards the effects of television on children and adolescents. A provisional subject index is provided to aid orientation and make it possible to find cross-connections between separate sub-divisions. Wherever it was possible or sensible, a distinction was made between literature on special research subjects and the original research reports. Introductory or synoptic literature has been included in cases where it contributes toward a general understanding of the fields of research with which we are concerned, even if it does not deal specifically with problems of television and children/ adolescents.

The enquiries which the IZI continuously receives clearly indicate that there is a wide range of interest in the television behaviour of and media effects on children, especially on preschool- and school-children on the one hand, and on adolescents on the other.

An attempt has therefore been made to separate studies on children from those on adolescents, the transition from childhood to adolescence having been placed at about the age of 12/13. Studies comparing different age groups have been arranged under the same heading.

All titles have been arranged in alphabetical order within the various chapters and sub-divisions, according to the name of the author mentioned first, or according to the subject title. Following the established rules of German documentation centres, works with a cooperative authorship of more than three writers are listed under the subject title, followed by the authors who are referred to as "Coll.", i. e. collaborators. Journal articles are cited with title of the journal, volume/year/issue, pages (e. g. Journal of Communication, 26/1976/2, pp. 1—13)..

The editors would be grateful for any corrections or additions, not to mention critical comments on the usefulness (or lack of it) of this type of reference book.

Manfred Meyer
Ursula Nissen

1. BIBLIOGRAPHIES

1

Bibliography of Nordic mass communication literature. Document list 1976.
Nordicom (Ed.)
Aarhus: Nordicom 1977. X, 118 pp.

Bibliography of Nordic mass communication literature. Index 1976.
Nordicom (Ed.)
Aarhus: Nordicom 1977. 65 pp.

2

Bibliography of works on mass communication published by Scandinavian
scholars in English and list of Scandinavian communication researchers.
Nordicom, Tampere (Ed.)
Tampere: Nordicom 1975. 64 pp.

3

Cantin, Hélène
Bibliographie. Etudes canadiennes sur les mass media.
Bibliography. Some writings on the Canadian mass media. Reprinted.
Université Laval, Quebec, Département de Journalisme (Ed.); Canadian Radio-
Television Commission (Ed.)
Ottawa: Information Canada 1975. 99 pp.

4

Carlsson, Ulla
Mass communication researchers in Sweden. Swedish mass communication
research. Publications in English, French and German.
Nordicom, Göteborg (Ed.)
Tampere: Nordicom 1978. 29 pp.

5

Children and television. An abstract bibliography.
Urbana, Ill.: ERIC Clearinghouse on Early Childhood Education 1975. 61 pp.

6

Comstock, George; Fisher, Marylin
Television and human behavior. A guide to the pertinent scientific literature.
Santa Monica, Ca.: Rand 1975. 344 pp.

7

Comstock, George
Television and human behavior. The key studies.

Christen, F. G. (Coll.); Fisher, M. L. (Coll.); Quarles, R. C. (Coll.); Richards, W. D. (Coll.)
Santa Monica, Ca.: Rand 1975. 251 pp.

8
Comstock, George; Lindsey, Georg
Television and human behavior. The research horizon, future and present.
Fisher, Marylin (Coll.)
Santa Monica, Ca.: Rand 1975. 120 pp.

9
CTW research bibliography. Research papers relating to the Children's Television Workshop and its experimental educational series: "Sesame Street" and "The Electric Company", 1968–76.
Children's Television Workshop, New York, Research Division (Ed.)
New York, N. Y.: Research Div., Children's Television Workshop n. d. (1976 or 1977). 20 pp.

10
Ellis, Connie
Current British research on mass media and mass communication. Register of ongoing and recently completed research.
Leicester: Leicester Documentation Centre for Mass Communication Research, Centre for Mass Communication Research, Univ. of Leicester 1976. 74 pp.

11
Ellis, Connie
Current British research on mass media and mass communication. Register of ongoing and recently completed research. Sept. 1977.
Leicester: Leicester Documentation Centre for Mass Communication Research, Centre for Mass Communication Research, Univ. of Leicester 1977. 77 pp.

12
Fairman, Edith M.
The effects of television violence on children. A selected annotated bibliography.
Washington, D. C.: Library of Congress, Congressional Research Service 1973. 14 pp.

13
Gordon, Thomas F.; Verna, Mary Ellen
Mass media and socialization. A selected bibliography.
Philadelphia, Pa.: Temple University, Radio-Television-Department 1973. 47 pp.

14
Kato, Hidetoshi
Japanese research on mass communication. Selected abstracts.
Honolulu: University Press of Hawaii, East-West Communication Institute
1974. 128 pp.

15
The list of works on mass communication by Scandinavian scholars in English.
Rev. edition.
Nordicom, Tampere (Ed.)
Tampere: Nordicom 1976. 21 pp.

16
Mensing, Katharina-Maria; Ubbens, Wilbert; Müller, Dagulf D.
Literaturverzeichnis Massenkommunikation. Mit einer Auswahlbibliographie
zum Thema Bildungstechnologie.
(Bibliography on mass communication. With a specialized bibliography on the
subject of educational technology.)
Verlag Volker Spiess, Berlin (Ed.); Gemeinschaftswerk der Evangelischen Pu-
blizistik, Frankfurt/M. (Ed.)
Berlin: Spiess 1975. 71 pp.

17
Meyer, Manfred; Nissen, Ursula
Bibliographie zu Sesame Street.
(Bibliography listing publications on Sesame Street.)
In: Fernsehen und Bildung, 10/1976/1–2, pp. 134–146.

18
Murray, John P.; Nayman, Oguz B.; Atkin, Charles K.
Television and the child. A comprehensive research bibliography.
In: Journal of Broadcasting, 16/1971–72/1, pp. 3–20.

19
Pisarek, Walery
Mass media and socialization. A selected international bibliography.
In: Mass media and socialization.
    Halloran, James D. (Ed.)
    Leicester: International Association for Mass Communication Research
    1976, pp. 57–116.

20
Scandinavian mass communication research. Publications in English, French and German.
Nordicom, Tampere (Ed.)
Tampere: Nordicom 1978. 45 pp.

21
A selection of communications bibliographies. Section 12.
In: Aspen handbook on the media. 1977–79 edition. A selective guide to research, organisations and publications in communications.
Rivers, William L. (Ed.) et al.
New York, London: Praeger 1977, pp. 371–396.

22
Sparks, Kenneth R.
A bibliography of doctoral dissertations in television and radio.
Syracuse, N. Y.: School of Journalism, Newhouse Communications Center, Syracuse University 1971. 119 pp.

23
Sterling, Christopher H.
Broadcasting and mass communication. A survey bibliography. 6th ed.
Philadelphia, Pa.: Temple Univ., Department of Radio-TV-Film 1976. 31 pp.

24
Television and social behavior. An annotated bibliography of research focusing on television's impact on children.
Atkin, Charles K. (Ed.); Murray, John P. (Ed.); Nayman, Oguz B. (Ed.)
United States Department of Health, Education, and Welfare (Ed.)
Washington, D. C.: U. S. Government Printing Office 1971. 150 pp.
(Arlington, Va.: ERIC ED 056 478)

25
Ubbens, Wilbert
Jahresbibliographie Massenkommunikation 1974–1975. Systematisches Verzeichnis der in den Jahren 1974 und 1975 innerhalb und außerhalb des Buchhandels veröffentlichten Literatur zu Presse, Rundfunk, Fernsehen, Film und angrenzenden Problemen.
(Annual bibliography on mass communication 1974–75. A systematic listing of publications on the press, radio, television, film and relative problems, published in 1974 and 1975 within and outside the booktrade.)
Bremen: Universität Bremen 1976. 209 pp.

26
Ubbens, Wilbert
Kommentierendes Verzeichnis von Textsammlungen und Vielverfasserschriften zur Massenkommunikation.
(A list of readers and publications with several authors on mass communication, with comment.)
In: Gesellschaftliche Kommunikation und Information, Bd. 2.
Aufermann, Jörg (Ed.) et al.
Frankfurt, M.: Athenäum Fischer Taschenb. Verl. 1973, pp. 776–799.

27
Welzel, Susanne
Literaturverzeichnis Massenmedien. Ausgewählte deutschsprachige Veröffentlichungen mit Annotationen.
(A bibliography on mass media. A selection of German publications with annotations.)
Wissenschaftliches Institut für Jugend- und Bildungsfragen in Film und Fernsehen, München (Ed.); Nordrhein-Westfalen, Min. für Wissenschaft und Forschung (Ed.); Landeszentrale für politische Bildung, Düsseldorf (Ed.)
München: Arbeitszentrum Jugend Film Fernsehen 1976. 94 pp.

2. MASS COMMUNICATION RESEARCH: INTRODUCTIONS, REVIEWS, READERS

28
Bledjian, Frank; Stosberg, Krista
Analyse der Massenkommunikation: Wirkungen.
(Analysis of mass communication: Effects.)
Düsseldorf: Bertelsmann Univ. Verl. 1972. 242 pp.

29
Böckelmann, Frank
Theorie der Massenkommunikation. Das System hergestellter Öffentlichkeit,
Wirkungsforschung und gesellschaftliche Kommunikationsverhältnisse.
(Theory of mass communication. The system of „produced" public, effects
research and the situation of social communication.)
Frankfurt, M.: Suhrkamp 1975. 310 pp.

30
Chaney, David
Processes of mass communication. New perspectives in sociology.
London: Macmillan 1972. 188 pp.

31
Current perspectives in mass communication research.
Kline, F. Gerald (Ed.); Tichenor, Phillip J. (Ed.)
Beverly Hills, Ca.: Sage 1972. 320 pp.

32
DeFleur, Melvin L.; Ball-Rokeach, Sandra
Theories of mass communication. 3rd. ed.
New York, N. Y.: McKay 1975. 288 pp.

33
Dröge, Franz; Weissenborn, Rainer; Haft, Henning
Wirkungen der Massenkommunikation.
(Effects of mass communication.)
Frankfurt, M.: Athenäum Fischer Taschenb. Verl. 1973. 208 pp.

34
Edelstein, Alex S.
An alternative approach to the study of source effects in mass communication.
In: Studies of Broadcasting 1973

Eguchi, H. (Ed.) et al.
Tokyo: Nippon Hoso Kyokai 1973, pp. 5–29.

35
The effects of television.
Halloran, James D. (Ed.)
London: Panther Books 1970. 224 pp.

36
Einführung in die Massenkommunikationsforschung.
(Introduction to mass communication research.)
Maletzke, Gerhard (Ed.)
Berlin: Spiess 1972. 187 pp.

37
Elliot, Philip
Uses and gratifications research. A critique and a sociological alternative.
In: The uses of mass communications. Current perspectives on gratifications
   research.
   Blumler, Jay G. (Ed.) et al.
   Beverly Hills, Ca.: Sage 1974, pp. 249–268.

38
Feldmann, Erich
Theorie der Massenmedien. Eine Einführung in die Medien- und Kommunika-
tionswissenschaft.
(A theory of mass media. Introduction to media and communication science.)
München: Reinhardt 1972. 245 pp.

39
Fujitake, Akira
Some comments on the studies of the effects of mass media of communication.
In: Studies of Broadcasting 1973.
   Eguchi, H. (Ed.) et al.
   Tokyo: Nippon Hoso Kyokai 1973, pp. 113–120.

40
Gesellschaftliche Kommunikation und Information. Forschungsrichtungen und
Problemstellungen. Ein Arbeitsbuch zur Massenkommunikation, I.
(Societal communication and information. Fields of research and problems. A
work-book in mass communication. I.)
Aufermann, Jörg (Ed.); Bohrmann, Hans (Ed.); Sülzer, Rolf (Ed.)
Frankfurt, M.: Athenäum Fischer Taschenb. Verl. 1973. 420 pp.

41
Gesellschaftliche Kommunikation und Information. Forschungsrichtungen und Problemstellungen. Ein Arbeitsbuch zur Massenkommunikation, II.
(Societal communication and information. Fields of research and problems. A work-book in mass communication. II.)
Aufermann, Jörg (Ed.); Bohrmann, Hans (Ed.); Sülzer, Rolf (Ed.)
Frankfurt, M.: Athenäum Fischer Taschenb. Verl. 1973. 873 pp.

42
Gordon, Thomas F.
Mass media and socialization. Theoretic approaches. Paper presented at the Annual Meeting of the International Communication Association, New Orleans, April 17–20, 1974.
n. p.: n. pr. 1974. 53 pp.
(Arlington, Va.: ERIC ED 097 733)

43
Grundfragen der Kommunikationsforschung. 5. Aufl.
(Basic problems of communication research.)
Schramm, Wilbur (Ed.)
München: Juventa 1973. 191 pp.
German edition of:
The science of human communication.
Schramm, Wilbur (Ed.)
New York, N.Y.: Basic Books 1963.

44
Hackforth, Josef
Massenmedien und ihre Wirkungen.
(Mass media and their effects.)
Göttingen: Schwartz 1976. 191, LXXXV pp.

45
Handbook of communication.
DeSola Pool, Ithiel (Ed.); Frey, Frederick W. (Ed.); Schramm, Wilbur (Ed.) et al.
Chicago, Ill.: Rand McNally College Publ. Comp. 1973. IX, 1011 pp.

46
Hyman, Herbert E.
Mass communication and socialization.
In: Public Opinion Quarterly, 37/1973–74/4, pp. 524–538.

47
Katz, Elihu; Gurevitch, Michael; Haas, Hadassah
On the use of the mass media for important things.
In: American Sociological Review, 38/1973/2, pp. 164–181.
Also in: Studies of Broadcasting 1973.
    Eguchi, H. (Ed.) et al.
    Tokyo: Nippon Hoso Kyokai 1973, pp. 31–65.

48
Katz, Elihu; Blumler, Jay G.; Gurevitch, Michael
Uses and gratifications research.
In: Public Opinion Quarterly, 37/1973–74/4, pp. 509–523.

49
Katz, Elihu; Blumler, Jay G.; Gurevitch, Michael
Uses of mass communication by the individual.
In: Mass communication research. Major issues and future directions.
    Davison, W. Phillips (Ed.) et al.
    New York, N. Y.: Praeger 1974, pp. 11–35.

50
Katz, Elihu; Blumler, Jay G.; Gurevitch, Michael
Utilization of mass communication by the individual.
In: The uses of mass communications. Current perspectives on gratifications
    research.
    Blumler, Jay G. (Ed.) et al.
    Beverly Hills, Ca.: Sage 1974, pp. 19–32.

51
Liebert, Robert M.; Schwartzberg, Neala S.
Effects of mass media.
In: Annual Review of Psychology, 28/1977/–, pp. 141–173.

52
Lyle, Jack
Television in daily life. Patterns of use. Overview.
In: Television and social behavior. Reports and papers.
    Vol. IV: Television in day-to-day life. Patterns of use.
    Rubinstein, Eli A. (Ed.) et al.
    Washington, D. C.: U. S. Government Printing Office 1972, pp. 1–32.

53
McCron, Robin
Changing perspectives in the study of mass media and socialization.
In: Mass media and socialization.
  Halloran, James D. (Ed.)
  Leicester: International Association for Mass Communication Research
  1976, pp. 13–44.

54
McQuail, Denis
Alternative models of television influence.
In: Children and television.
  Brown, Ray (Ed.)
  London: Cassell and Collier Macmillan 1976, pp. 343–360.

55
McQuail, Denis
Soziologie der Massenkommunikation.
(Sociology of mass communication.)
Berlin: Spiess 1973. 122 pp.
German edition of:
McQuail, Denis
Towards a sociology of modern communications.
New York, N. Y.: Macmillan 1969.

56
McQuail, Denis; Blumler, Jay G.; Brown, J. R.
The television audience. A revised perspective.
In: Sociology of mass communications.
  McQuail, Denis (Ed.)
  Harmondsworth: Penguin Books 1972, pp. 135–165.

57
Maletzke, Gerhard
Ziele und Wirkungen der Massenkommunikation.
(Objectives and effects of mass communication.)
Hamburg: Hans-Bredow-Institut 1976. VII, 294 pp.

58
Mass communication and society.
Curran, James (Ed.); Gurevitch, Michael (Ed.); Woollacott, Janet (Ed.) et al.
Open University (Ed.)
London et al.: Arnold 1977. 479 pp.

59

Mass communications and youth. Some current perspectives.
Kline, F. Gerald (Ed.); Clarke, Peter (Ed.)
Beverly Hills, Ca.: Sage 1971. 128 pp.

60

Mass communication research. Major issues and future directions.
Davison, W. Phillips (Ed.); Yu, Frederick T. C. (Ed.)
New York, N. Y.: Praeger 1974. 246 pp.

61

Mass media and communication. 2nd ed., rev., enl.
Steinberg, Charles S. (Ed.)
New York, N. Y.: Hastings House Publ. 1972. 686 pp.

62

Mass media and society. 2nd ed.
Wells, Alan (Ed.)
Palo Alto, Ca.: Mayfield 1975. 412 pp.

63

Massenkommunikationsforschung 1: Produktion.
(Mass communication research 1: Production.)
Prokop, Dieter (Ed.)
Frankfurt, M.: Fischer Taschenb. Verl. 1972. 424 pp.

64

Massenkommunikationsforschung 2: Konsumtion.
(Mass communication research 2: Consumption.)
Prokop, Dieter (Ed.)
Frankfurt, M.: Fischer Taschenb. Verl. 1973. 500 pp.

65

Media sociology. A reader. 3rd ed.
Tunstall, Jeremy (Ed.)
London: Constable 1974. 574 pp.

66

Noelle-Neumann, Elisabeth
Return to the concept of powerful mass media.
In: Studies of Broadcasting 1973.
    Eguchi, H. (Ed.) et al.
    Tokyo: Nippon Hoso Kyokai 1973, pp. 67–102.

67
Pietilä, Veikko
Gratifications and content choices in mass media uses.
Tampere: Univ. of Tampere, Research Institute 1974. 79 pp.

68
Political communication. Issues and strategies for research.
Chaffee, Steven H. (Ed.)
Beverly Hills, Ca.: Sage 1975. 319 pp.

69
The process and effects of mass communication. 3rd ed.
Schramm, Wilbur (Ed.); Roberts, Donald F. (Ed.)
Urbana, Ill.: Univ. of Illinois 1974. 997 pp.

70
Pross, Harry
Medienforschung. Film, Funk, Fernsehen, Presse.
(Media research. Film, radio, television, press.)
Darmstadt: Habel 1972. 303 pp.

71
Renckstorf, Karsten
Alternative Ansätze der Massenkommunikationsforschung. Wirkungs- vs. Nut-
zenansatz.
(Alternative approaches to mass communication research. Uses and gratifications
approach.)
In: Rundfunk und Fernsehen, 21/1973/2–3, pp. 183–197.

72
Renckstorf, Karsten
Neue Perspektiven in der Massenkommunikationsforschung. Beiträge zur Be-
gründung eines alternativen Forschungsansatzes.
(New perspectives in mass communication research. Contributions to the devel-
opment of an alternative research approach.)
Berlin: Spiess 1977. 194 pp.

73
Robinson, John P.
Toward defining the functions of television.
In: Television and social behavior. Reports and papers.
    Vol. IV: Television in day-to-day life. Patterns of use.

24

Rubinstein, Eli A. (Ed.) et al.
Washington, D. C.: U. S. Government Printing Office 1972, pp. 568–603.

74
Rosengren, Karl Erik; Windahl, Swen
Mass media consumption as a functional alternative.
In: Sociology of mass communications.
McQuail, Denis (Ed.)
Harmondsworth: Penguin Books 1972, pp. 166–194.

75
Rosengren, Karl Erik; Windahl, Swen
Funktionale Aspekte bei der Nutzung der Massenmedien.
(Functional aspects of the use of mass media.)
In: Einführung in die Massenkommunikationsforschung.
Maletzke, Gerhard (Ed.)
Berlin: Spiess 1972, pp. 169–186.

76
Schenk, Michael
Publikums- und Wirkungsforschung. Theoretische Ansätze und empirische Befunde der Massenkommunikationsforschung.
(Audience and effects research. Theoretical approaches and empirical findings of mass communication research.)
Tübingen: Mohr 1978. XI, 292 pp.

77
Schramm, Wilbur
Men, messages, and media. A look at human communication.
New York, N. Y.: Harper and Row 1973. 341 pp.

78
Silbermann, Alphons; Krüger, Udo Michael
Soziologie der Massenkommunikation.
(Sociology of mass communication.)
Stuttgart: Kohlhammer 1973. 136 pp.

79
Sozialisation durch Massenkommunikation. Der Mensch als soziales und personales Wesen. Bd. IV.
(Socialization through mass communication. Man as a social and personal being.)

Ronneberger, Franz (Ed.)
Stuttgart: Enke 1971. 440 pp.

80
Sociology of mass communications. Selected readings.
McQuail, Denis (Ed.)
Harmondsworth: Penguin Books 1972. 477 pp.

81
Teichert, Will
Bedürfnisstruktur und Mediennutzung. Fragestellung und Problematik des "uses and gratifications approach".
(The structure of needs and the use of media. The "uses and gratifications approach" – the question and the problems.)
In: Rundfunk und Fernsehen, 23/1975/3–4, pp. 269–283.

82
Teichert, Will
‚Fernsehen' als soziales Handeln. Zur Situation der Rezipientenforschung. Ansätze und Kritik.
(Watching television as social action. On the present state of recipient research. Approaches – criticism.)
In: Rundfunk und Fernsehen, 20/1972/4, pp. 421–439.

83
Teichert, Will
‚Fernsehen' als soziales Handeln (II). Entwürfe und Modelle zur dialogischen Kommunikation zwischen Publikum und Massenmedien.
(Watching television as social action (II). Communication as dialogue between the audience and the mass media. Propositions and models.)
In: Rundfunk und Fernsehen, 21/1973/4, pp. 356–382.

84
Uses and gratifications studies. Theory and methods.
Stockholm: Sveriges Radio Audience and Programme Research Department 1973. 179 pp.

85
The uses of mass communications. Current perspectives on gratifications research.
Blumler, Jay G. (Ed.); Katz, Elihu (Ed.)
Beverly Hills, Ca.: Sage 1974. 318 pp.

86
Weiss, Walter
Mass communication.
In: Annual Review of Psychology, 22/1971/–, pp. 309–336.

87
Wright, Charles R.
Mass communication. A sociological perspective. Second edition.
New York: Random House 1975. 180 pp.

3. TELEVISION, CHILDREN AND ADOLESCENTS: GENERAL INTRODUCTORY WORKS, LITERATURE REVIEWS

88
Abruzzini, Pompeo
Television and the socialization of children.
In: Der Anteil der Massenmedien bei der Herausbildung des Bewußtseins in der sich wandelnden Welt. Konferenzprotokoll I.
Sektion Journalistik, Karl-Marx-Univ. (Ed.)
Leipzig: Sektion Journalistik, Karl-Marx-Univ. 1974, pp. 207–213.

89
Allouche-Benayoun, B. Joëlle
Der Einfluß des bewegten Bildes auf Kinder und Jugendliche. Französische Forschungen von 1970–1975.
In: Fernsehen und Bildung, 9/1975/2–3, S. 229–249.

Allouche-Benayoun, B. Joëlle
The influence of moving pictures on children and young people. French research activities from 1970–1975.
In: Fernsehen und Bildung (special English issue), 9/1975/2–3, pp. 137–157.

90
Allouche-Benayoun, B. Joëlle
Processus de socialisation et influence de l'image filmée sur les enfants et les jeunes.
(Socialization processes and the influence of the moving picture on children and adolescents.)
In: Bulletin de psychologie, 29/1975–76/321, 4–7, pp. 243–254.

91
Allouche-Benayoun, B. Joëlle
Recherches françaises (1970–1975).
(French research 1970–1975).
In: Les cahiers de l'animation, –/1977/15–16, pp. 117–130.

92
Anderson, Daniel R.
Children's attention to television. Paper presented at the Biennial Meeting of the Society for Research in Child Development, New Orleans, Louisiana, March 17–20, 1977.
n. p.: n. pr. 1977. 14 pp.
(Arlington, Va.: ERIC ED 136 958)

93
Baran, Stanley J.; Meyer, Timothy P.
Imitation and identification. Two compatible approaches to social learning from the electronic media.
In: AV communication review, 22/1974/2, pp. 167–179.

94
Baran, Stanley J.
Television and social learning in the institutionalized MR.
In: Mental Retardation, 11/1973/3, pp. 36–38.

95
Baranowski, Marc D.
Television and the adolescent.
In: Adolescence, 6/1971/–, pp. 369–396.

96
Bergler, R.; Six, B.
Die Wirkungen des Fernsehens auf Kinder und Jugendliche. Literaturübersicht und Sammelreferat.
(The effects of television on children and adolescents. Bibliography and review paper.)
Arbeitsgemeinschaft Rundfunkwerbung (Ed.); Zweites Deutsches Fernsehen (Ed.); ZAW-Fachausschuß für Rundfunkwerbung (Coll.)
Frankfurt, M.: Arbeitsgemeinschaft Rundfunkwerbung 1975. 119 pp.

97
Bryan, James H.; Schwartz, Tanis
Effects of film material upon children's behavior.
In: Psychological Bulletin, 75/1971, pp. 50–59.

98
Children and television.
Brown, Ray (Ed.)
London: Cassell and Collier Macmillan 1976. 368 pp.

99
Children's research at Sveriges Radio.
Faith-Ell, Peggy (Coll.); Feilitzen, Cecilia von (Coll.); Filipson, Leni (Coll.) et al.
Stockholm: Sveriges Radio Audience and Programme Research Dept. 1976. 10 pp.

100
Collins, W. Andrew
The developing child as a viewer. The effects of television on children and adolescents.
In: Journal of Communication, 25/1975/4, pp. 35–44.

101
Comstock, George
Effects of television on children: what is the evidence?
Santa Monica, Ca.: Rand 1975. 16 pp.

102
Comstock, George
The evidence so far. The effects of television on children and adolescents.
In: Journal of Communication, 25/1975/4, pp. 25–34.

103
Comstock, George
The long-range impact of television. Paper presented at American Association for Public Opinion Research and World Association for Public Opinion Research, Asheville, N. C., May 13–16, 1976.
Santa Monica, Ca.: Rand Corp. 1976. 11 pp.
(Arlington, Va.: ERIC ED 134 164)

104
Comstock, George
Television and the teacher.
Santa Monica, Ca.: Rand 1976. 15 pp.

105
Cramond, Joyce
Introduction of TV and effects upon children's daily lives.
In: Children and television.
    Brown, Ray (Ed.)
    London: Cassell and Collier Macmillan 1976, pp. 267–284.

106
DeDomenico, Francesco
Die Forschungen der RAI zu Fernsehen, Familie und kindlicher Sozialisation.
In: Fernsehen und Bildung, 9/1975/2–3, pp. 190–207.

DeDomenico, Francesco
RAI Audience Research Study Programme on television, family, and children socialization.
In: Fernsehen und Bildung (special English issue), 9/1975/2-3, pp. 100-116.

107
Epstein, Robert H.
Language learning from television. What is known and what is needed?
n. p.: n. pr. 1976. 40 pp.
(Arlington, Va.: ERIC ED 134 332)

108
Feeley, Joan T.
Television and reading in the seventies. Paper presented at the Annual Meeting of the International Reading Association, 19th. New Orleans, May 1-4, 1974.
n. p.: n. pr. 1974. 14 pp.
(Arlington, Va.: ERIC ED 089 258)

109
Feilitzen, Cecilia von; Linné, Olga
Children and identification in the mass communication process. A summary of Scandinavian research and a theoretical discussion.
Stockholm: Sveriges Radio, Audience and Programme Research Department 1974. 39 pp.

110
Feilitzen, Cecilia von
Children and television in the socialization process. Some results of Scandinavian research.
Stockholm: Sveriges Radio 1975-1976. 33 pp. (Pub. No. 28/1975-1976)

Also published as:
Feilitzen, Cecilia von
Findings of Scandinavian research on child and television in the process of socialization.
In: Fernsehen und Bildung (special English issue), 9/1975/2-3, pp. 54-84.

Feilitzen, Cecilia von
Ergebnisse skandinavischer Forschungen zum Thema Kind und Fernsehen im Sozialisationsprozeß.
In: Fernsehen und Bildung, 9/1975/2-3, pp. 143-175.

111

Feilitzen, Cecilia von; Linné, Olga
Identifying with television characters. The effects of television on children and adolescents.
In: Journal of Communication, 25/1975/4, pp. 51–55.

112

Fernsehen und Bildung, Jahrgang 9, Heft 2–3.
Fernsehen und Sozialisationsprozesse in der Familie.
Internationales Zentralinstitut für das Jugend- und Bildungsfernsehen, München (Ed.)
München: IZI 1975. 284 pp.

Fernsehen und Bildung, Vol. 9 (1975) 2/3. Special English Issue.
Television and socialization processes in the family.
Internationales Zentralinstitut für das Jugend- und Bildungsfernsehen, München (Ed.)
München: IZI 1976. 192 pp.

113

Grewe-Partsch, Marianne
Bericht über Forschungsarbeiten in Israel und Japan zu Sozialisationsprozessen durch Fernsehen in der Familie.
In: Fernsehen und Bildung, 9/1975/2–3, pp. 224–229.

Grewe-Partsch, Marianne
Report on some research activities in Israel and Japan on socialization processes in the family by television.
In: Fernsehen und Bildung (special English issue), 9/1975/2–3, pp. 132–147.

114

Halloran, James D.
On the research approaches for studying socialization in the family. An outline from Great Britain.
In: Fernsehen und Bildung (special English issue), 9/1975/2–3, pp. 15–25.

Halloran, James D.
Über die Ansätze zur Erforschung der Sozialisation in der Familie. Ein Überblick aus Großbritannien.
In: Fernsehen und Bildung, 9/1975/2–3, pp. 98–110.

115

Halloran, James D.
The social effects of television.

In: The effects of television.
    Halloran, James D. (Ed.)
    London: Panther Books 1970, pp. 25–68.

116
Hatano, Giyoo
Recent Japanese studies on "TV and the child".
In: International Studies of Broadcasting.
    Eguchi, H. (Ed.) et al.
    Tokyo: Nippon Hoso Kyokai 1971, pp. 157–179.

117
Howe, Michael J. A.
Television and children.
London: New University Education 1977. 157 pp.

118
Howitt, Dennis
The effects of television on children.
In: Children and television.
    Brown, Ray (Ed.)
    London: Cassell and Collier Macmillan 1976, pp. 320–342.

119
Hüther, Jürgen
Sozialisation durch Massenmedien. Ziele, Methoden, Ergebnisse einer medien-
bezogenen Jugendkunde.
(Socialization through the mass media. Objectives, methods, and results of
media-related youth research.)
Opladen: Westdeutscher Verl. 1975. 175 pp.

120
Jakab, Zoltán
Ungarische Untersuchungen zur Sozialisation von Kindern und Jugendlichen im
Hinblick auf das Fernsehen.
In: Fernsehen und Bildung, 9/1975/2–3, pp. 208–224.

Jakab, Zoltán
Hungarian studies on socialization of children and young people for television.
In: Fernsehen und Bildung (special English issue), 9/1975/2–3, pp. 117–132.

121
Kinder vor dem Bildschirm.
(Children in front of the TV screen.)
Heygster, Anna-Luise (Ed.); Stolte, Dieter (Ed.)
Mainz: v. Hase & Koehler 1974. 240 pp.
Mainzer Tage der Fernseh-Kritik VI.

122
Kniveton, Bromley H.
Social learning and imitation in relation to TV.
In: Children and television.
  Brown, Ray (Ed.)
  London: Cassell and Collier Macmillan 1976, pp. 237–266.

123
Krugmann, Herbert E.; Hartley, Eugene L.
Passive learning from television.
In: Public Opinion Quarterly, 34/1970/1, pp. 184–190.

124
Leifer, Aimée Dorr; Gordon, Neal J.; Graves, Sherryl Browne
Children's television: More than mere entertainment.
In: Harvard Educational Review, 44/1974/2, pp. 213–245.

125
Leifer, Aimée Dorr; Gordon, Neal J.; Graves, Sherryl Browne
Le programme des recherches américaine.
(The American research programme.)
In: Les cahiers de l'animation, –/1977/15–16, pp. 91–104.

126
Leifer, Aimée Dorr
Research on the socialization influence of television in the United States.
In: Fernsehen und Bildung (special English issue), 9/1975/2–3, pp. 26–53.

Leifer, Aimée Dorr
Untersuchungen über die Sozialisationseinflüsse des Fernsehens in den Ver-
einigten Staaten.
In: Fernsehen und Bildung, 9/1975/2–3, pp. 111–143.

127
Leifer, Aimée Dorr
Television and the development of social behavior.

In: The developing individual in a changing world.
  Vol. II: Social and environmental issues.
  Riegel, Klaus F. (Ed.) et al.
  The Hague: Mouton 1976, pp. 495–503.

128
Liebert, Robert M.; Neale, John M.; Davidson, Emily S.
The early window. Effects of television on children and youth.
New York, N. Y.: Pergamon Press 1973. 193 pp.

129
Liebert, Robert M.; Poulos, Rita W.
Television and personality development. The socializing effects of an entertainment medium.
In: Child personality and psychopathology. Current topics. Vol. 2.
  Davids, A. (Ed.)
  New York, N Y.: Wiley 1975, pp. 61–97.

130
Liebert, Robert M.; Poulos, Rita W.
Television as a moral teacher.
In: Moral development and behavior. Theory, research, and social issues.
  Lickona, Thomas (Ed.)
  New York, N. Y.: Holt, Rinehart and Winston 1976, pp. 284–298.

131
Murray, John P.
Beyond entertainment. Television's effects on children and youth.
n. p.: n. pr. 1976. 27 pp.
(Arlington, Va.: ERIC ED 131 856)

132
Noble, Grant
Children in front of the small screen.
London: Constable; Beverly Hills, Ca.: Sage 1975. 256 pp.

133
Roberts, Donald F.; Schramm, Wilbur
Children's learning from the media.
In: The process and effects of mass communication.
  Schramm, Wilbur (Ed.)
  Urbana, Ill.: Univ. of Illinois Press 1971, pp. 596–611.

134
Roberts, Donald F.
Communication and children. A development approach.
In: Handbook of communication.
   DeSola Pool, Ithiel (Ed.) et al.
   Chicago: Rand McNally Publ. Comp. 1973, pp. 174–215.

135
Saxer, Ulrich
Forschungen im deutschsprachigen Raum zum Thema Fernsehen und Sozialisa-
tionsprozesse in der Familie.
In: Fernsehen und Bildung, 9/1975/2–3, pp. 175–190.

Saxer, Ulrich
Contributions of research in the German-language areas to the subject: Tele-
vision and socialization in the family.
In: Fernsehen und Bildung (special English issue), 9/1975/2–3, pp. 85–100.

136
Searcy, Ellen; Chapman, Judith
The status of research in children's television.
Interagency Panel on Early Childhood Research and Development (Ed.)
Washington, D. C.: Interagency Panel 1972. 142 pp.
(Arlington, Va.: ERIC ED 086 355)

137
Searle, Ann
Children's perception and understanding of television.
Plymouth Polytechnic, Department of Behavioural and Social Science (Ed.)
Plymouth, Devon: Plymouth Polytechnic 1975. 18 pp.

138
Stein, Aletha H.; Friedrich, Lynette K.
Impact of television on children and youth.
Chicago, Ill.: University of Chicago Press 1975. 72 pp.

139
Stein, Aletha H.
Mass media and young children's development.
In: Early childhood education. The Seventy-first Yearbook of the National Society
   for the Study of Education, Part II.
   Gordon, Ira J. (Ed.) et al.
   Chicago, Ill.: University of Chicago Press 1972, pp. 181–202.

140
Sturm, Hertha
The application of Piaget's criteria to television programmes for children.
In: Information programmes for children 7 to 12 years old.
Werner, Peter (Ed.)
Geneva: European Broadcasting Union 1977, pp. 12–19.

141
Sturm, Hertha
Les effets émotionnels de la télévision sur les enfants.
(The emotional effects of television on children.)
Marly-le-Roi: Institut National d'Education Populaire, Dépt. des Etudes de la
Recherche et de la Documentation 1977, pp. 111–116.
In: Les cahiers de l'animation, –/1977/15–16.

142
Sturm, Hertha
Fernsehen und Entwicklung der Intelligenz. Kritische Überlegungen zu medien-
spezifischen Sozialisationswirkungen.
(Television and the development of intelligence. Critical remarks on the subject
of media specific socialization effects.)
In: Sozialisation durch Massenkommunikation, Bd. V.
Ronneberger, Franz (Ed.) et al.
Stuttgart: Enke 1971, pp. 290–304.

143
Sturm, Hertha
Die Forschungen des Internationalen Zentralinstituts für das Jugend- und Bil-
dungsfernsehen.
In: Fernsehen und Bildung, 9/1975/2–3, pp. 249–254.

Sturm, Hertha
The research activities of the Internationales Zentralinstitut für das Jugend-
und Bildungsfernsehen.
In: Fernsehen und Bildung (special English issue), 9/1975/2–3, pp. 158–163.

144
Wackman, Daniel B.; Wartella, Ellen
A review of cognitive development theory and research and the implication
for research on children's responses to television.
In: Communication Research, 4/1977/2, pp. 203–224.

4. STUDIES ON THE USES AND FUNCTIONS OF TELEVISION AND OTHER MEDIA

4.1 Comparisons of various age groups, developmental studies

145
Bessler, Hansjörg; Zimmer-Schürings, Margot
Lebensgewohnheiten von Kindern. Auswertung einer Stichtagbefragung von Kindern in Fernsehhaushalten.
(The life styles of children. Evaluation of a survey of children in TV households.)
In: Das Fernsehen und sein Publikum.
    Stolte, Dieter (Ed.)
    Mainz: v. Hase u. Köhler 1973, pp. 202–295.

146
Brown, J. Ray
Children's uses of television.
In: Children and television.
    Brown, Ray (Ed.)
    London: Cassell and Collier Macmillan 1976, pp. 116–136.

147
Brown, J. Ray
Warum Kinder das Fernsehen und andere Medien nutzen.
(Why children use television and other media.)
In: Media-Perspektiven, –/1977/3, pp. 142–155.

148
Children and television.
A survey of the role of TV in children's experience, and of parents' attitudes towards TV for their children.
Independent Broadcasting Authority, Audience Research Department, London (Ed.)
London: Independent Broadcasting Authority 1974. 61 pp., Appx.

149
Children and television.
Main findings from Shizuoka survey 1967.
Takeshima, Y. (Coll.); Tada, T. (Coll.); Fujioka, H. (Coll.); Kikuchi, N. (Coll.) et al.
Radio and Television Culture Research Institute, Tokyo (Ed.)
Tokyo: Nippon Hoso Kyokai 1971. 40 pp.

150
Children as viewers and listeners.
A study by the BBC for its General Advisory Council.
British Broadcasting Corporation, London (Ed.)
London: British Broadcasting Corp. 1974. 35 pp.

151
Children's view. National survey, week 9–78, 27th February – 5th March 1978.
Independent Broadcasting Authority, Audience Research Department, London (Ed.)
London: Independent Broadcasting Authority 1978. 8 pp.

152
Corset, Pierre
Les jeunes enfants et la télévision.
(Young children and television.)
Meyer, Georges (Coll.)
In: Télévision et éducation, –/1972/28, pp. 7–71.

153
Darschin, Wolfgang
Kinder vor dem Bildschirm. Erste Ergebnisse der teleskopie-Fernsehforschung.
(Children in front of television. First results of teleskopie television research.)
In: Media Perspektiven, –/1976/8, pp. 366–370.

154
Darschin, Wolfgang
Veränderungen im Fernsehkonsum der Kinder. Neue Ergebnisse aus der kontinuierlichen Zuschauerforschung.
(Changes in children's TV consumption. New results from continuous audience research.)
In: Media Perspektiven, –/1977/11, pp. 613–624.

155
Feilitzen, Cecilia von
The functions served by the media. Report on a Swedish study.
In: Children and television.
    Brown, Ray (Ed.)
    London: Cassell and Collier Macmillan 1976, pp. 90–115.

156
Frank, Bernward
Kinder vor dem Bildschirm. Sehgewohnheiten und Sehinteressen.
(Children in front of the screen. Viewing habits and program interests.)
In: Kinder vor dem Bildschirm.
    Heygster, Anna-Luise (Ed.) et al.
    Mainz: v. Hase und Köhler 1974, pp. 49–75.

157
Furu, Takeo
The function of television for children and adolescents.
Nakano, Terumi (Coll.); Furuhata, Kazutaka (Coll.); Akutsu, Yoshihiro (Coll.)
et al.
Tokyo: Sophia University 1971. 323 pp.

158
Greenberg, Bradley S.
Gratifications of television viewing and their correlates for British children.
In: The uses of mass communications. Current perspectives on gratifications
    research.
    Blumler, Jay G. (Ed.) et al.
    Beverly Hills, Ca.: Sage 1974, pp. 71–92.

159
Greenberg, Bradley S.
Viewing and listening parameters among British youngsters.
In: Journal of Broadcasting, 17/1973/2, pp. 173–188.

    Also in:
    Children and television.
    Brown, Ray (Ed.)
    London: Cassell and Collier Macmillan 1976, pp. 29–44.

160
Horn, Imme
Kinder und Fernsehen. Neuere Untersuchungsergebnisse zum Fernsehverhalten
von 3- bis 9jährigen.
(Children and television. Recent results of research on the viewing behavior of
three to nine year-olds.)
In: Media Perspektiven, –/1976/8, pp. 357–366.

161
Lometti, Guy E.; Reeves, Byron; Bybee, Carl R.
Investigating the assumptions of uses and gratifications research.
In: Communication Research, 4/1977/4, pp. 321–338.

162
Lyle, Jack; Hoffman, Heidi R.
Children's use of television and other media.
In: Television and social behavior. Reports and papers.
    Vol. IV: Television in day-to-day life. Patterns of use.
    Rubinstein, Eli A. (Ed.) et al.
    Washington, D. C.: U. S. Government Printing Office 1972, pp. 129–256.

163
Lyle, Jack; Hoffman, Heidi R.
Television in the daily lives of our children. Paper presented at the Symposium
"The early window. The role of television in childhood" at the Annual Meeting
of the American Psychological Association, Washington, D. C., Sept. 4, 1971.
n. p.: n. pr. 1971. 20 pp.
(Arlington, Va.: ERIC ED 053 575)

164
Regional differences in children's appreciation of programmes.
Independent Broadcasting Authority, Audience Research Dept., London (Ed.)
London: IBA 1977. 12 pp.

165
Rubin, Alan M.
Television usage, attitudes and viewing behaviors of children and adolescents.
In: Journal of Broadcasting, 21/1977/3, pp. 355–369.

166
Smith, David M.
Children, mass media and excitement. An empirical study.
In: Gazette, 23/1977/2, pp. 116–133.

167
Steinmann, Matthias
Kind und Fernsehen. Eine Studie über das Fernseh- und Freizeitverhalten der
Kinder in der Schweiz. 2. Aufl.
(Children and television. A study on viewing and leisure time behaviour of
children in Switzerland. 2nd ed.)

Schweizerische Radio- und Fernsehgesellschaft, Zürich (Ed.)
Zürich: Schweizerische Radio- und Fernsehgesellschaft 1974. 62 pp., Appx.

168
Use of the mass media by the urban poor. Findings of three research projects, with an annotated bibliography.
Greenberg, Bradley S. (Ed.); Dervin, Brenda (Ed.); Dominick, Joseph R. (Coll.); Bowes, John (Coll.)
New York, N. Y.: Praeger 1970. XVI, 251 pp.

169
Validating techniques for measuring children's appreciation of programmes.
Independent Broadcasting Authority, Audience Research Department, London (Ed.)
London: Independent Broadcasting Authority 1977. 16 pp.

170
Werner, Anita
Children and television in Norway.
In: Gazette, 17/1971/3, pp. 133–151.

4.2 Preschool children

171
Annis, Phyllis M.
Research into TV and the pre-school child.
In: Educational Media International, –/1974/4, pp. 13–19.

172
Dunn, Gwen
The box in the corner. Television and the under-fives. A study.
New York et al.: The Macmillan Press 1977. VIII, 157 pp.

173
Dunn, Gwen
Television and the preschool child.
London: Independent Television Authority 1974. 206 pp.

174
Epstein, Robert H.; Bozler, Dianne A.
Project in television and early childhood education at the University of Sou-

thern California. A study of preschool children's television viewing behavior and circumstances.
Annenberg School of Communications, Los Angeles, Calif. (Ed.); School for Early Childhood Education, Los Angeles, Calif. (Ed.)
Los Angeles, Calif.: Annenberg School of Communications, School for Early Childhood Education, Univ. of Southern Calif. 1976. 20 pp.
(Arlington, Va.: ERIC ED 134 329)

175
Filipson, Leni
The role of radio and TV in the lives of pre-school children. Summary.
Swedish Broadcasting Corp., Audience and Programme Research Department, Stockholm (Ed.)
Stockholm: Swedish Broadcasting Corp. 1976. 39 pp.

176
Firnkes, Marita; Keilhacker, Margarete; Vogg, Günther
Das Fernsehen im Vorschulalter. Empirische Studie über Funktion und Wirkung des Fernsehens bei Kindern im Vorschulalter. 2. überarb. Aufl.
(Television in the preschool age. Empirical study on the function and effect of television on preschool children. 2nd rev. ed.)
München: Wissenschaftliches Institut für Jugend- und Bildungsfragen in Film und Fernsehen 1973. 162 pp.

177
Gadberry, Sharon
Television as baby-sitter. A field comparison of preschoolers' behavior during playtime and during television viewing.
In: Child Development, 45/1974/-, pp. 1132-1136.

178
Liikanen, Pirkro
The use of TV-programmes and other materials in the Finnish Kindergarten
In: Educational Media International, -/1974/4, pp. 6-13.

179
Lyle, Jack; Hoffman, Heidi R.
Explorations in patterns of television viewing by preschool-age children.
In: Television and social behavior. Reports and papers.
    Vol. IV: Television in day-to-day life. Patterns of use.
    Rubinstein, Eli A. (Ed.) et al.
    Washington, D. C.: U. S. Government Printing Office 1972, pp. 257-273.

180
Lyle, Jack; Hoffman, Heidi R.
Television viewing by pre-school-age children.
In: Children and television.
  Brown, Ray (Ed.)
  London: Cassell and Collier Macmillan 1976, pp. 45–61.

181
Prawat, Dorothy M.; Prawat, Richard S.
Preschooler's viewing behavior while watching two types of television fare.
In: Perceptual and Motor Skills, 40/1975/–, pp. 575–582.

182
Rydin, Ingegerd
Children's understanding of television. Pre-school children's perception of an informative programme.
Swedish Broadcasting Corp., Stockholm, Audience and Programme Research Department (Ed.)
Stockholm: Swedish Broadcasting Corp. 1976. 36 pp. Appx.

183
Stevenson, Harold W.
Television and the behavior of preschool children.
In: Television and social behavior. Reports and papers.
  Vol. II: Television and social learning.
  Murray, John P. (Ed.) et al.
  Washington, D. C.: U. S. Government Printing Office, 1972, pp. 346–371.

184
Vorschulkinder und Fernsehen. Empirische Untersuchungen in drei Ländern.
Hömberg, Erentraud (Ed.); Stiftung Prix Jeunesse (Ed.)
München u. a.: Verl. Dokumentation 1978. 78 pp.

English edition:
Pre-school children and television. Two studies carried out in three countries.
Hömberg, Erentraud (Ed.); Stiftung Prix Jeunesse (Ed.)
New York: Saur 1978. 78 pp.

4.3 School children (elementary and intermediate grades)

185
Akutsu, Yoshihiro
Opinion leadership in children's television behavior.

In: Furu, Takeo
    The function of television for children and adolescents.
    Tokyo: Sophia Univ. 1971, pp. 270–281.

186
Brown, J. Ray; Cramond, Joyce K.; Wilde, Robert J.
Displacement effects of television and the child's functional orientation to media.
In: The uses of mass communication.
    Blumler, Jay G. (Ed.) et al.
    Beverly Hills, Ca.: Sage 1974, pp. 93–112.

187
Childers, Perry R.; Ross, James
The relationship between viewing television and student achievement.
In: Journal of Educational Research, 66/1973/7, pp. 317–319.

188
Crawford, Patricia; Rapoport, Max
Results of a survey of pupils and teachers regarding television.
North York, Board of Education (Ed.)
Willowdale, Ontario: North York, Board of Education 1976. 58 pp.
(Arlington, Va.: ERIC ED 127 976)

189
Feeley, Joan T.
Children's content interest. A factor analytic study. Paper presented at the Annual Meeting of the National Council of Teachers of English (62nd, Minneapolis, Minnesota, November 23–25, 1972).
n. p.: n. pr. 1972. 18 pp.
(Arlington, Va.: ERIC ED 094 389)

190
Feeley, Joan T.
Interest patterns and media preferences of middle-grade children.
In: Reading World, 13/1974/3, pp. 224–237.

191
Greenberg, Bradley S.; Ericson, Philip M.; Vlahos, Mantha
Children's television behaviors as perceived by mother and child.
In: Television and social behavior. Reports and papers.
    Vol. IV: Television in day-to-day life. Patterns of use.

Rubinstein, Eli A. (Ed.) et al.
Washington, D. C.: U. S. Government Printing Office 1972, pp. 395–409.

German translation:
Greenberg, Bradley S.; Ericson, Philip M.; Vlahos, Mantha
Kinder vor dem Fernsehschirm – in der Beurteilung durch Mütter und Kinder.
In: Rundfunk und Fernsehen, 20/1972/1, pp. 123–137.

192
Greenberg, Bradley S.; Dominick, Joseph R.
Television behavior among disadvantaged children.
In: Use of the mass media by the urban poor.
Greenberg, Bradley S. (Ed.) et al.
New York, N. Y.: Praeger 1970, pp. 51–72.

193
Hagmann, Thomas
Fernsehen im Leben der Kinder. Mit Ergebnissen einer schweizerischen Untersuchung.
(Television in the lives of children. With results of a Swiss study.)
Bern: Haupt 1972. 89 pp.

194
Harper, D.; Munro, Joan; Himmelweit, Hilde T.
Social and personality factors associated with children's tastes in television viewing.
In: Media sociology. A reader. 3rd ed.
Tunstall, Jeremy (Ed.)
London: Constable 1970, pp. 363–371.
Also in:
Second progress report and recommendations.
Television Research Committee (Ed.)
Leicester: Leicester University Press 1969, pp. 55–63.

196
Hunziker, Peter; Kohli, Martin; Lüscher, Kurt
Fernsehen im Alltag der Kinder. Eine Voruntersuchung.
(Television in the everyday life of children. A preliminary study.)
In: Rundfunk und Fernsehen, 21/1973/4, pp. 383–405.

197
Jaronik, Catherine
A study of the influence of outside interests, other mass media, grade level and sex on children's television viewing and program preferences.

DuVall, Charles R. (Coll.)
South Bend, Ind.: Indiana Univ. 1975. 122 pp.

198
Long, Barbara H.; Henderson, Edmund H.
Children's use of time. Some personal and social correlates.
In: Elementary School Journal, 73/1973/4, pp. 193–199.

199
Murray, John P.; Kippax, Susan
Children's social behavior in three towns with differing television experience.
In: Journal of Communication, 28/1978/1, pp. 19–29.

200
Murray, John P.; Kippax, Susan
Television and social behavior in three communities. A field experiment.
In: Australian Journal of Psychology, 29/1977/1, pp. 31–43.

201
Murray, John P.; Kippax, Susan
Television diffusion and social behaviour in three communities. A field experiment.
n. p.: n. pr. 1976. 19 pp., 10 pp. n. pag.
(Arlington, Va.: ERIC ED 131 855)

202
Murray, John P.
Television in inner-city homes. Viewing behavior of young boys.
In: Television and social behavior. Reports and papers.
    Vol. IV: Television in day-to-day life. Patterns of use.
    Rubinstein, Eli A. (Ed.) et al.
    Washington, D. C.: U. S. Government Printing Office 1972, pp. 345–394.

203
Powell, R. J.
Television viewing by young secondary students. A study of the television viewing behavior of children at form two level.
Australian Broadcasting Control Board (Ed.)
Melbourne: Australian Broadcasting Control Board 1971. 34 pp.
(Arlington, Va.: ERIC ED 054 622)

204
Starkey, John D.; Swinford, Helen Lee
Reading? Does television viewing time affect it?
n. p.: n. pr. 1974. 12 pp.
(Arlington, Va.: ERIC ED 090 966)

206
Streicher, Lawrence H.; Bonney, Norman L.
Children talk about television.
Chicago, Ill.: Institute for Juvenile Research 1974. 27 pp.
(Arlington, Va.: ERIC ED 095 850)
Also in:
Journal of Communication, 24/1974/3, pp. 54–61.

207
Striefel, Sebastian
Isolating variables which affect TV preferences of retarded children.
In: Psychological Reports, 35/1974/1, pp. 115–122.

208
Striefel, Sebastian; Smeets, Paul M.
TV preference as a technique for selection of reinforcers.
In: Psychological Reports, 35/1974/1, pp. 107–113.

209
Williams, Frederick
Social class differences in how children talk about television.
In: Advances in communication research.
    Mortensen, David (Ed.) et al.
    New York, N. Y.: Harper and Row 1973, pp. 398–406.

4.4 Adolescents

210
Adolescents' TV relations. Three scales.
Rosengren, Karl Erik (Coll.); Windahl, Swen (Coll.); Hakansson, Per-Arne
(Coll.); Johnsson-Smaragdi, Ulla (Coll.)
In: Communication Research, 3/1976/4, S. 347–366.

211
Arafat, Ibtihaj S.; Hulbert, James M.; Filmer, Paul A.
Academic achievement and television viewing. The case of the college student.

Paper presented at the Southern Sociological Society annual meeting, Atlanta, April 18, 1974.

n. p.: n. pr. 1974. 21 pp.

(Arlington, Va.: ERIC ED 119 637)

212

Bechtel, Robert B.; Achelpohl, Clark; Akers, Roger

Correlates between observed behavior and questionnaire responses on television viewing.

In: Television and social behavior. Reports and papers.

Vol. IV: Television in day-to-day life. Patterns of use.

Rubinstein, Eli A. (Ed.) et al.

Washington, D. C.: U. S. Government Printing Office 1972, pp. 274–344.

213

Blizard, John

Individual differences and television viewing behavior.

Mayborough, Victoria: Hedges and Bell 1972. 119 pp.

214

Brodlie, Jerome F.

Drug abuse and television viewing patterns.

In: Psychology, 9/1972/2, pp. 33–36.

215

Chaffee, Steven H.; McLeod, Jack M.

Adolescent television use in the family context.

In: Television and social behavior. Reports and papers.

Vol. III: Television and adolescent agressiveness.

Comstock, George A. (Ed.) et al.

Washington, D. C.: U. S. Government Printing Office 1972, pp. 149–172.

216

Chaffee, Steven H.; Tims, Albert R.

Interpersonal factors in adolescent television use.

In: Journal of Social Issues, 32/1976/4, pp. 98–115.

217

Chaffee, Steven H.; McLeod, Jack M.; Atkin, Charles K.

Parental influences on adolescent media use.

In: Mass communications and youth. Some current perspectives.

Kline, Gerald F. (Ed.) et al.

Beverly Hills, Ca.: Sage 1971, pp. 21–38.
Also in:
American Behavioral Scientist, 14/1971/3, pp. 323–340.

218
Cronen, Vernon
Belief, salience, media exposure, and summation theory.
In: Journal of Communication, 23/1973/1, pp. 86–94.

219
Danowski, James A.
Alternative information theoretic measures of television messages. An empirical
test. Paper presented at the Annual Meeting of the Association for Education in
Journalism, 57th, San Diego, Cal., Aug. 18–21, 1974.
n. p.: n. pr. 1974. 30 pp.
(Arlington, Va.: ERIC ED 096 686)

220
Dembo, Richard
Gratifications found in media by British teenage boys.
In: Journalism Quarterly, 50/1973/–, pp. 517–526.

221
Dembo, Richard
Life style and media use among English working-class youth.
In: Gazette, 18/1972/1, pp. 24–36.

222
Dembo, Richard; McCron, Robin
Social factors in media use.
In: Children and television.
    Brown, Ray (Ed.)
    London: Cassell and Collier Macmillan 1976, pp. 137–166.

223
Dominick, Joseph R.; Greenberg, Bradley S.
Mass media functions among low-income adolescents.
In: Use of the mass media by the urban poor.
    Greenberg, Bradley S. (Ed.) et al.
    New York, N. Y.: Praeger 1970, pp. 31–49.

224
Frank, Bernward
Jugend und Fernsehen. Verhaltensweisen und Einstellungen jugendlicher Fernsehzuschauer.
(Young people and television. Behavior and attitudes of adolescent TV viewers.)
In: Zweites Deutsches Fernsehen
    Jahrbuch 1971.
    Mainz: Zweites Deutsches Fernsehen 1972, pp. 192–196.

225
Frank, Bernward
Tagesablauf und Mediennutzung der jugendlichen und erwachsenen Fernsehzuschauer.
(Time budget and the use of media – adolescent and adult TV viewers.)
In: Das Fernsehen und sein Publikum. Studien zum Tagesablauf 1970/71.
    Stolte, Dieter (Ed.)
    Mainz: v. Hase und Köhler 1973, pp. 67–199.

226
Hein, Jürgen
Massenmedien und Leseinteressen.
(Mass media and reading interests.)
In: Schule und Medien. Beiträge zur empirischen Unterrichts- und Erziehungsforschung.
    Rutt, Theodor (Ed.) et al.
    Ratingen: Kastellaun 1974, pp. 27–68.

227
Hendry, Leo B.; Patrick, Helen
Adolescents and television.
In: Journal of Youth and Adolescence, 6/1977/4, pp. 325–336.

228
Hendry, Leo B.; Thornton, J. E.
Games theory, television and leisure. An adolescent study.
In: British Journal of Social and Clinical Psychology, 15/1976/–, pp. 369–376.

229
Himmelweit, Hilde; Swift, Betty
Adolescent and adult media use and taste. A longitudinal study.
London: London School of Economics 1972. 85 pp.

230
Himmelweit, Hilde; Swift, Betty
Continuities and discontinuities in media usage and taste. A longitudinal study.
In: Journal of Social Issues, 32/1976/4, pp. 133–156.

231
Horn, Imme
Jugend und Fernsehen. Bericht über Einstellungen und Verhalten der 14- bis 24jährigen gegenüber dem Fernsehen.
(Young people and television. A report on attitudes and behavior of the 14 to 24 year-olds with respect to television.)
Mainz: Zweites Deutsches Fernsehen 1975. 64 pp.

232
Horn, Imme
Jugendliche urteilen über Jugendprogramme.
(Young people evaluate youth programmes.)
In: Zweites Deutsches Fernsehen
    Jahrbuch 1973.
    Mainz: Zweites Deutsches Fernsehen 1974, pp. 135–139.

233
Hornik, Robert C.
Mass media use and the 'revolution of rising frustration'. A reconsideration of the theory.
In: Communication Research, 4/1977/4, pp. 387–414.

234
Izcaray, Fausto; Allen, Richard; Coulter, Renee
Interpersonal communication pattern, mass media and the occupational expectation process. Paper presented at the Annual Meeting of the Association for Education in Journalism, 57th, San Diego, Calif., August 18–21, 1974.
n. p.: n. pr. 1974. 25 pp.
(Arlington, Va.: ERIC ED 096 656)

235
Johnstone, John W.
Social integration and mass media use among adolescents. A case study.
In: The uses of mass communications.
    Blumler, Jay G. (Ed.) et al.
    Beverly Hills, Ca.: Sage 1974, pp. 35–47.

236
Kabel, Rainer; Eckhardt, Josef
Interessen und Probleme von Jugendlichen und jungen Erwachsenen. Zwei Umfragen des SFB und des WDR.
(Interests and problems of adolescents and young adults. Two surveys by SFB and WDR.)
In: Media-Perspektiven, –/1977/3, pp. 131–141.

237
Kline, F. Gerald; Miller, Peter V.; Morrison, Andrew J.
Adolescents and family planning information. An exploration of audience needs and media effects.
In: The uses of mass communications.
  Blumler, Jay G. (Ed.) et al.
  Beverly Hills, Ca.: Sage 1974, pp. 113–136.

238
Klockhaus, Ruth
Befunde und motivationspsychologische Überlegungen zum Medienkonsum Jugendlicher.
(The media consumption of young people – findings and motivational questions.)
In: Communicatio Socialis, 9/1976/1, pp. 1–15.

239
Lohisse, Jean
Les jeunes et la radio-télévision.
(Young people and broadcasting.)
Bruxelles: Radio-Télévision Belgique 1970. 69 pp.

240
McLeod, Jack M.; Brown, Jane D.
The family environment and adolescent television use.
In: Children and television.
  Brown, Ray (Ed.)
  London: Cassell and Collier Macmillan 1976, pp. 199–233.

241
Muramatsu, Yasuko
Views of the Japanese youths towards television.
In: Studies of Broadcasting.
  Eguchi, H. (Ed.) et al.
  Tokyo: Nippon Hoso Kyokai 1975, pp. 39–61.

242
O'Keefe, Garrett J. Jr.; Spetnagel, H. T.
Patterns of college undergraduates' use of selected news media.
In: Journalism Quarterly, 50/1973/3, pp. 543–548.

243
Rust, Holger
Jugendliche und Gesellschaftsbilder im Fernsehen. Eine Fallstudie zur Rezeption neuerer Unterhaltungsprogramme.
(Young people and the images of society in television. A case study on the reception of some recent entertainment programmes.)
Berlin: Spiess 1978. 134 pp.

244
Smith, David M.
Some uses of mass media by 14 year olds.
In: Journal of Broadcasting, 16/1971–1972/1, pp. 37–50.

245
Surlin, Stuart H.; Dominick, Joseph
Television's function as a 'third parent' for black and white teen-agers.
In: Journal of Broadcasting, 15/1970–1971/1, pp. 55–64.

246
Two studies of mass media use by contemporary young adults.
Washington D. C.: American Newspaper Publishers Association 1974. pp. 1–20.
(Arlington, Va.: ERIC ED 117 702)

247
Wade, Serena E.
Adolescents, creativity, and media. An exploratory study.
In: Mass communications and youth. Some current perspectives.
    Kline, Gerald (Ed.) et al.
    Beverly Hills, Ca.: Sage 1971, pp. 39–49.
    Also in:
    American Behavioral Scientist, 14/1971/3, pp. 341–351.

248
Wade, Serena E.
Interpersonal discussion. A critical predictor of leisure activity.
In: Journal of Communication, 23/1973/4, pp. 426–445.

249
Zoll, Ralf; Henning, Eike
Massenmedien und Meinungsbildung. Angebot, Reichweite, Nutzung und Inhalt der Medien in der BRD.
(Mass media and the formation of opinion. Offering, coverage, use and content of media in the Federal Republic of Germany.)
München: Juventa 1970. 335 pp.

5. STUDIES ON COGNITIVE AND EMOTIONAL EFFECTS

5.1 Comparisons of various age groups, developmental studies

250
Baron, L.; O'Bryan, Kenneth G.
A developmental look at eye movement patterns of internally and externally controlled children watching two instructional models.
Toronto: Ontario Institute for Studies in Education 1974. 16 pp. n. pag.
(Arlington, Va.: ERIC ED 122 811)

251
Child versus adult perception of evaluative messages in verbal, vocal, and visual channels.
Bugental, Daphne E. (Coll.); Kaswan, Jaques W. (Coll.); Love, Leonore R. (Coll.); Fox, Michael N. (Coll.)
In: Developmental Psychology, 2/1970/3, pp. 367–375.

252
Collins, W. Andrew; Westby, Sally Driscoll
Children's processing of social information from televised dramatic programs.
Paper presented at the Biennal Meeting of the Society for Research in Child Development, Denver, Col., April 10–13, 1975.
n. p.: n. pr. 1975. 12 pp.
(Arlington, Va.: ERIC ED 113 024)

253
Collins, W. Andrew
Developmental aspects of understanding and evaluating television content.
Paper presented at the Biennial Meeting of the Society for Research in Child Development, Philadelphia, Pa., March 30, 1973.
n. p.: n. pr. 1973. 10 pp.
(Arlington, Va.: ERIC ED 075 096)

254
Collins, W. Andrew
Learning of media content. A developmental study.
In: Child Development, 41/1970/–, pp. 1133–1142.

255
Denney, Douglas R.
Modeling and interrogative strategies. Paper presented at the 82nd Annual Convention of the American Psychological Association, New Orleans, Louis., Sept. 1974.
n. p.: n. pr. 1974. 6 pp.
(Arlington, Va.: ERIC ED 103 102)

256
Developmental aspects of variables relevant to observational learning.
Leifer, Aimée Dorr (Coll.); Collins, W. Andrew (Coll.); Gross, Barbara M. (Coll.); Taylor, Peter H. (Coll.) et al.
In: Child Development, 42/1971/–, pp. 1509–1516.

257
Forte, Michael
Cognitive processes for evaluating the credibility of television content. Paper presented at the Annual Meeting of the American Psychological Association, Washington, D. C., September 5, 1975.
n. p.: n. pr. 1971. 9 pp.
(Arlington, Va.: ERIC ED 135 329)

258
Graves, Sherryl Browne
Content attended to in evaluating television's credibility. Paper presented at the Annual Meeting of the American Psychological Association, Washington, D. C., September 5, 1976.
n. p.: n. pr. 1976. 9 pp.
(Arlington, Va.: ERIC ED 135 330)

259
Graves, Sherryl Browne
Overview of the project. (Credibility of television content.) Paper presented at the Annual Meeting of the American Psychological Association, Washington, D. C., September 5, 1976.
n. p.: n. pr. 1976. 9 pp.
(Arlington, Va.: ERIC ED 135 331)

260
Grusec, Joan E.
Effects of co-observer evaluations on imitation. A developmental study.
In: Developmental Psychology, 8/1973/1, p. 141.

261
Hawkins, Robert P.
The dimensional structure of children's perception of television reality.
In: Communication Research, 4/1977/3, pp. 299–320.

262
Hawkins, Robert P.
Learning of peripheral content in film. A developmental study.
In: Child Development, 44/1973/–, pp. 214–217.

263
Klapper, Hope Lunin
Children's perceptions of the realism and unrealism of television. A pilot study.
Summary and analysis. Paper presented at the American Association for Public
Opinion Research, Lake George, N. Y., May 1974.
n. p.: n. pr. 1974, 18 pp.
(Arlington, Va.: ERIC ED 121 266)

264
Leifer, Aimée Dorr
Factors which predict the credibility ascribed to television. Paper presented at the
Annual Meeting of the American Psychological Association, Washington, D. C.,
September 5, 1976.
n. p.: n. pr. 1976. 15 pp.
(Arlington, Va.: ERIC ED 135 332)

265
Lemon, Judith
Teaching children to become more critical consumers of television. Paper presented
at the Annual Meeting of the American Psychological Association, Washington,
D. C., September 5, 1976.
n. p.: n. pr. 1976. 7 pp.
(Arlington, Va.: ERIC ED 135 333)

266
Phelps, Erin M.
Knowledge of the television industry and relevant first-hand experience.
Paper presented at the Annual Meeting of the American Psychological
Association, Washington, D. C., September 5, 1976.
n. p.: n. pr. 1976. 9 pp.
(Arlington, Va.: ERIC ED 135 334)

267
Reeves, Byron; Greenberg, Bradley S.
Children's perceptions of television characters. Paper presented at the Annual Meeting of the Association for Education in Journalism, College Park, Maryland, August 1976.
n. p.: n. pr. 1976. 20 pp., 8 pp. Appx.
(Arlington, Va.: ERIC ED 124 986)

268
Reeves, Byron; Greenberg, Bradley S.
Children's perception of television characters.
In: Human Communication Research, 3/1977/2, pp. 113–127.

269
Reeves, Byron; Miller, M. Mark
A multidimensional measure of children's identification with television characters.
In: Journal of Broadcasting, 22/1978/1, pp. 71–86.

5.2 Preschool children

270
Corder-Bolz, Charles; O'Bryant, Shirley
Teacher vs. program. Can people affect television?
In: Journal of Communication, 28/1978/1, pp. 97–103.

271
Deutsch, Francine
Female preschoolers' perceptions of affective responses and interpersonal behavior in videotaped episodes.
In: Developmental Psychology, 10/1974/5, pp. 733–740.

272
Dubanoski, Richard A.; Parton, David A.
Effect of the presence of a human model on imitative behavior in children.
In: Developmental Psychology, 4/1971/3, pp. 463–468.

273
Henderson, Ronald W.; Swanson, Rosemary
The effects of televised instruction and ancillary support system on the development of cognitive skills in Papago native-American children.

Tucson, Arizona: Arizona Center for Educational Research and Development, College of Education, Univ. of Arizona 1975. 99 pp., 88 pp. Appx. (Arlington, Va.: ERIC ED 119 628)

274
Henderson, Ronald W.; Swanson, Rosemary
The effects of televised skill instruction, instructional system support, and parental intervention on the development of cognitive skills. Final report.
Tucson, Arizona: Arizona Center for Educational Research and Development, College of Education, Univ. of Arizona 1977. I, 106 pp.

275
Henderson, Ronald W.; Swanson, Rosemary; Zimmerman, Barry J.
Inquiry response induction in preschool children through televised modeling.
In: Developmental Psychology, 11/1975/4, pp. 523–524.

276
Henderson, Ronald W.; Swanson, Rosemary; Zimmerman, Barry J.
Training seriation responses in young children through televised modeling of hierarchically sequenced rule components.
In: American Educational Research Journal, 12/1975/4, pp. 479–489.

277
Morris, Bridget
Children's response to pre-school television. A method of assessing the response of pre-school children to programmes made for them. Including a systematic analytical study of a sample of Inner Ring Birmingham Nursery School children.
London: Independent Television Authority 1975–1976. IV, 103 pp.

278
Neely, J. J.; Heckel, R. V.; Leichtman, H. M.
The effect of race of model and response consequences to the model on imitation in children.
In: Journal of Social Psychology, 89/1973/–, pp. 225–231.

279
Rydin, Ingegerd
Information processes in pre-school children.
1. How relevant and irrelevant verbal supplements affect retention of a factual radio program.

Sveriges Radio, Audience and Programme Research Department, Stockholm (Ed.)
Stockholm: Swedish Broadcasting Corporation, Audience and Programme
Research Dept. 1973. 22 pp., 13 pp. Appx.

280
Rydin, Ingegerd
Information processes in pre-school children.
2. The tale of the seed. Facts and irrelevant details in a TV-programme for
children.
Sveriges Radio, Audience and Programme Research Department, Stockholm (Ed.)
Stockholm: Swedish Broadcasting Corporation, Audience and Programme
Research Dept. 1976. II, 34 pp., 13 pp. Appx.

281
Singer, Jerome L.; Singer, Dorothy G.
Can TV stimulate imaginative play? Fostering creativity in children.
In: Journal of Communication, 26/1976/3, pp. 74–80.

282
Singer, Jerome L.; Singer, Dorothy G.
Fostering imaginative play in pre-school children. Effects of television viewing
and direct adult modeling. Paper to be presented at the Annual Meeting of the
American Psychological Association, New Orleans, Louis., Aug. 30–Sept. 3, 1974.
n. p.: n. pr. 1974. 46 pp.
(Arlington, Va.: ERIC ED 089 873)

283
Thelen, Mark H.
The effect of subject race, model race, and vicarious praise on vicarious
learning.
In: Child Development, 42/1971/–, pp. 972–977.

5.3 School children

284
Akamatsu, T. John; Thelen, Mark H.
The acquisition and performance of a socially neutral response as a function of
vicarious reward.
In: Developmental Psychology, 5/1971/3, pp. 440–445.

285
Baran, Stanley J.; Meyer, Timothy P.
Retarded children's perceptions of favorite television characters as behavioral models.
In: Mental Retardation, 13/1975/4, pp. 28–31.

286
Baran, Stanley J.
Television programs as socializing agents for mentally retarded children.
In: AV Communication Review, 25/1977/3, pp. 281–289.

287
Chandler, Michael J.; Greenspan, Stephen; Barenboim, Carl
Judgments of intentionality in response to videotaped and verbally presented moral dilemmas. The medium is the message.
In: Child Development, 44/1973/–, pp. 315–320.

288
Denis, Michel
La mémoire d'un message filmique comparée à celle d'un message verbal chez des enfants d'age scolaire.
(Memory retention of a filmed message compared to a verbal message in school age children.)
In: Journal de Psychologie Normale et Pathologique, 68/1971/1, pp. 69–87.

289
Denney, Douglas R.
Modeling and eliciting effects upon conceptual strategies.
In: Child Development, 43/1972/–, pp. 810–823.

290
Denney, Douglas R.
Modeling effects upon conceptual style and cognitive tempo.
In: Child Development, 43/1972/–, pp. 105–119.

291
Expectancy to perform and vicarious reward: their effects upon imitation.
Thelen, Mark H. (Coll.); Rennie, David L. (Coll); Fryrear, Jerry L. (Coll.); McGuire, Dennis (Coll.)
In: Child Development, 43/1972/–, pp. 699–703.

292
Greenberg, Bradley S.; Reeves, Byron
Children and the perceived reality of television.
In: Journal of Social Issues, 32/1976/4, pp. 86–97.

293
Greenberg, Bradley S.; Reeves, Byron
Children's reactions to TV blacks.
In: Journalism Quarterly, 49/1972/1, pp. 5–14.

294
Koblewska, Janina
Results of Polish researches into the influence of TV film heroes on school-children.
In: Educational Media International, –/1972/2, pp. 17–23.

295
Lahtinen, Pauli; Taipale, Hannu
The effects of TV on children's drawings and vocabulary.
n. p.: Institute for Educational Research, Univ. of Jyväskylä 1971. 22 pp.

296
Meline, Caroline W.
Does the medium matter? Fostering creativity in children.
In: Journal of Communication, 26/1976/3, pp. 81–89.

297
Meyer, Timothy
Children's perceptions of favorite television characters as behavioral models.
In: Educational Broadcasting Review, 7/1973/1, pp. 25–33.

298
Musgrave, Peter W.; Reid, George R.
Some measures of children's values.
In: Social Science Information, 10/1971/1, pp. 137–153.

299
O'Bryan, Kenneth G.
Eye movements as an index of television viewing strategies. Paper presented at the Biennial Meeting of the Society for Research in Child Development, Denver, Col., April 10–13, 1975.
n. p.: n. pr. 1975. 20 pp.
(Arlington, Va.: ERIC ED 115 391)

300
Ridberg, Eugene H.; Parke, Ross D.: Hetherington, E. Mavis
Modification of impulsive and reflective cognitive styles through observation of
film-mediated models.
In: Developmental Psychology, 5/1971/3, pp. 369–377.

301
Salomon, Gavriel
Cognitive effects of visual media.
In: The developing individual in a changing world.
    Vol. II: Social and environmental issues.
    Riegel, Klaus F. (Ed.) et al.
    The Hague: Mouton 1976, pp. 487–494.

302
Salomon, Gavriel; Cohen, Akiba A.
Television formats, mastery of mental skills, and the acquisition of knowledge.
In: Journal of Educational Psychology, 69/1977/5, pp. 612–619.

303
Stern, Stanley L.
Television and creativity. The effect of viewing certain categories of commer-
cial television broadcasting on the divergent thinking abilities of intellectually
gifted elementary students.
Los Angeles, Ca., Univ. of Southern California, School of Education, Ph. D.
diss., 1973. 154 pp.
(Arlington, Va.: ERIC ED 082 496)

304
Thelen, Mark H.
Long-term retention of verbal imitation.
In: Developmental Psychology, 3/1970/1, pp. 29–31.

305
Wolf, Thomas M.
Response consequences to televised modeled sex-inappropriate play behavior.
In: Journal of Genetic Psychology, 127/1975/–, pp. 35–44.

306
Yates, Gregory C. R.
Influence of televised modeling and verbalization on children's delay of
gratification.
In: Journal of Experimental Child Psychology, 18/1974/2, pp. 333–339.

5.4 Adolescents

307
Baran, Stanley J.
Sex on TV and adolescent sexual self-image.
In: Journal of Broadcasting, 20/1976/1, pp. 61–68.

308
Baxter, Leslie A.; Bittner, John R.
High school and college student perceptions of media credibility.
In: Journalism Quarterly, 51/1974/3, pp. 517–520.

309
Berg, Charles M.; Infante, Dominic A.
The impact of music modality on the perception of moving images. Paper presented at the Annual Meeting of the International Communication Association, Portland, Or., April 14–17, 1976.
n. p.: n. pr. 1976. 26 pp.
(Arlington, Va.: ERIC ED 122 335)

310
Cantor, Joanne R.; Mody, Bella; Zillmann, Dolf
Residual emotional arousal as a distractor in persuasion.
In: Journal of Social Psychology, 92/1974/–, pp. 231–244.

311
Cumberbatch, Guy; Howitt, Dennis
Identification with aggressive television characters and children's moral judgments.
In: Determinants and origins of aggressive behavior.
    DeWit, Jan (Ed.) et al.
    The Hague: Mouton 1974, pp. 517–523.

312
Donohue, Thomas R.
Favorite TV characters as behavioral models for the emotionally disturbed.
In: Journal of Broadcasting, 21/1977/3, pp. 333–345.

313
Donohue, Thomas R.
Viewer perceptions of color and black-and-white paid political advertising.
In: Journalism Quarterly, 50/1973/–, pp. 660–665.

314
Donohue, Thomas R.; Donohue, William A.
Viewer response sets to filmed and video taped television content. Paper presented at the Annual Meeting of the Eastern Communication Association, New York City, March 24–26, 1977.
n. p.: n. pr. 1977. n. pag. (15 pp.).
(Arlington, Va.: ERIC ED 137 850)

315
Glass, David C.; Gordon, Andrew; Henchy, Thomas
The effects of social stimuli on psychophysiological reactivity to an averse film.
In: Psychonomic Science, 20/1970/4, pp. 255–256.

316
Howitt, Dennis; Cumberbatch, Guy
The parameters of attraction to mass media figures.
In: Journal of Moral Education, 2/1973/3, pp. 269–281.
    Also in:
    Children and television
    Brown, Ray (Ed.)
    London: Cassell and Collier Macmillan 1976, pp. 167–183.

317
Jugend und Fernsehen. Eine internationale Untersuchung über die Urteile der Juries, die Intentionen der Produzenten und die Reaktionen junger Zuschauer, dargelegt am Beispiel Prix Jeunesse 1970 "Man in Metropolis" und "Baff".
(Young people and television. An international study of juries, producers and their young audiences based on the prize-winning programmes of Prix Jeunesse 1970: 'Man in Metropolis' and 'Baff'.)
Kyrantonis, Dorothee (Coll.); Vonhoff, Renate (Coll.)
Internationales Zentralinstitut für das Jugend- und Bildungsfernsehen (Ed.)
München: Internationales Zentralinstitut für das Jugend- und Bildungsfernsehen 1972. 173 pp.

318
Katzman, Natan; Nyenhuis, James
Color vs. black-and-white effects on learning, opinion, and attention.
In: AV Communication Review, 20/1972/1, pp. 16–28.

319
Kunce, Joseph T.; Thelen, Mark H.
Modeled standards of self-reward and observer performance.
In: Developmental Psychology, 7/1972/2, pp. 153–156.

320
Miller, William C.; Beck, Thomas
How do TV-parents compare to real parents?
In: Journalism Quarterly, 53/1976/2, pp. 324–328.

321
Morris, Larry W.; Spiegler, Michael D.; Liebert, Robert M.
Effects of a therapeutic modeling film on cognitive and emotional components
of anxiety.
In: Journal of Clinical Psychology, 30/1974/–, pp. 219–223.

322
Rosenbaum, William B.; Rosenbaum, Leonard L.; McGinnies, Elliott
Sex differences in selective exposure.
In: Journal of Social Psychology, 92/1974/–, pp. 85–89.

323
Scherer, Klaus R.
Stereotype change following exposure to counter-stereotypical media heroes.
In: Journal of Broadcasting, 15/1971/4, pp. 91–100.

324
Stevenson, Harold W.; Friedrichs, Ann G.; Simpson, William E.
Learning and problem solving by the mentally retarded under three testing
conditions.
In: Developmental Psychology, 3/1970/3, pp. 307–312.

325
Sturm, Hertha; Holzheuer, Katharina; Helmreich, Reinhard
Emotionale Wirkungen des Fernsehens. Jugendliche als Rezipienten.
(Emotional effects of television. Young people as recipients.)
Berghaus, Margot (Coll.)
München u. a.: Verl. Dokumentation Saur 1978. 128 pp.

326
Thelen, Mark H.; Fryrear, Jerry L.
Effect of observer and model race on the imitation of standards of self-reward.
In: Developmental Psychology, 5/1971/1, pp. 133–135.

327
Toomey, Tim C.
Alteration of perceptual mode correlate through a televised model.
In: Journal of Experimental Research in Personality, 6/1972/–, pp. 52–59.

328
Ward, Scott; Ray, Michael L.
Cognitive responses to mass communication. Results from laboratory studies and a field experiment. Paper presented at the Annual Meeting of the Association for Education in Journalism, 57th, San Diego, Ca., August 18–21, 1974.
n. p.: n. pr. 1974. 28 pp.
(Arlington, Va.: ERIC ED 095 578)

329
Weigel, Russell H.; Jessor, Richard
Television and adolescent conventionality. An exploratory study.
In: Public Opinion Quarterly, 37/1973/–, pp. 77–90.

330
Wilson, Edward C.
The effect of medium on loss of information.
In: Journalism Quarterly, 51/1974/1, pp. 111–115.

331
Zeigler, Sherilyn K.
Attention factors in televised messages. Effects on looking behavior and recall.
In: Journal of Broadcasting, 14/1970/3, pp. 307–315.

6. STUDIES ON ASPECTS OF SOCIALIZATION

6.1 Socialization and interaction in the family context

332
Abel, John D.
The family and child television viewing.
In: Journal of Marriage and the Family, 38/1976/2, pp. 331–335.

333
Barcus, F. Earle
Concerned parents speak out on children's television.
Boston, Mass.: Action for Children's Television 1973. 103 pp.
(Arlington, Va.: ERIC ED 084 860)

334
Brown, J. Ray
Child socialization: the family and television.
In: Der Anteil der Massenmedien bei der Herausbildung des Bewußtseins in der
sich wandelnden Welt.
Konferenzprotokoll II.
Sektion Journalistik, Karl-Marx-Univ., Leipzig (Ed.)
Leipzig: Sektion Journalistik, Karl-Marx-Univ. 1974, pp. 235–241.

335
Brown, J. Ray; Linné, Olga
The family as a mediator of television's effects.
In: Children and television.
Brown, Ray (Ed.)
London: Cassell and Collier Macmillan 1976, pp. 184–198.

336
Dimmick, John
Family communication and TV program choice.
In: Journalism Quarterly, 53/1976/4, pp. 720–723.

337
Familie und Fernsehen. Neueste Ergebnisse der Fernsehforschung und deren Konse-
quenzen für die Programmarbeit.
(Family and television. Latest results of television research and their consequences
for programme work.)
Kellner, Hella (Coll.); Frank, Bernward (Coll.)

Zweites Deutsches Fernsehen, Mainz (Ed.)
Mainz: Zweites Deutsches Fernsehen 1978. 55 pp.

338
Hunziker, Peter; Lüscher, Kurt; Fauser, Richard
Fernsehen im Alltag der Familie.
(Television in the everyday life of the family.)
In: Rundfunk und Fernsehen, 23/1975/3–4, pp. 284–315.

339
Hunziker, Peter
Fernsehen und interpersonelle Kommunikation in der Familie.
(Television and interpersonal communication in the family.)
In: Publizistik, 21/1976/2, pp. 180–195.

340
Hunziker, Peter
Television and interpersonal communication in the family.
In: Der Anteil der Massenmedien bei der Herausbildung des Bewußtseins in der
    sich wandelnden Welt.
    Konferenzprotokoll II.
    Sektion Journalistik, Karl-Marx-Univ., Leipzig (Ed.)
    Leipzig: Sektion Journalistik, Karl-Marx-Univ. 1974, pp. 285–293.

341
Kniveton, Bromley H.
Maternal concepts of the impact of television on young boys.
In: Durham Research Review, 29/1972/–, pp. 673–677.

342
Kohli, Martin
Der Einfluß der Situation auf die Rezeption einer Fernsehsendung durch Kinder.
Eine experimentelle Pilot-Studie.
(The influence of the situational context on children's reception of a TV film.
An experimental pilot study.)
Konstanz: Universität, Fachgruppe Soziologie 1975. 94 pp.

343
Kohli, Martin
The influence of the situational context on children's reception of a TV film.
In: Der Anteil der Massenmedien bei der Herausbildung des Bewußtseins in der
    sich wandelnden Welt.

Konferenzprotokoll II.
Sektion Journalistik, Karl-Marx-Univ., Leipzig (Ed.)
Leipzig: Sektion Journalistik, Karl-Marx-Univ. 1974, pp. 305–313.

344
McLeod, Jack M.; Brown, Jane D.
The family environment and adolescent television use.
In: Children and television.
  Brown, Ray (Ed.)
  London: Cassell and Collier Macmillan 1976, pp. 199–233.

345
Martin, Cora A.; Benson, Leonard
Parental perceptions of the role of television in parent-child interaction.
In: Journal of Marriage and the Family, 32/1970/–, pp. 410–414.

346
Rossiter, John R.; Robertson, Thomas S.
Children's television viewing. An examination of parent-child consensus.
In: Sociometry, 38/1975/2, pp. 308–326.

347
Schäfer, Harald
Struktur-Untersuchungen zur Situation der Familie vor und auf dem Bildschirm.
(Structural research on the family situation in front of and on the screen.)
Marburg: Marburger Studienkreis für Europäische Ethnologie 1973. 209 pp.

348
Smith, David M.
Mass media as a basis for interaction. An empirical study.
In: Journalism Quarterly, 52/1975/1, pp. 44–49, 105.

6.2 Role socialization (sex roles, occupational roles)

349
Cheles-Miller, Pamela
An investigation of whether the stereotypes of husband and wife presented in television commercials can influence a child's perception of the role of husband and wife. Paper presented at the Annual Meeting of the International Communication Association, New Orleans, April 17–20, 1974.
n. p.: n. pr. 1974. 13 pp.
(Arlington, Va.: ERIC ED 094 439)

350
Cheles-Miller, Pamela
Reactions to marital roles in commercials.
In: Journal of Advertising Research, 15/1975/4, pp. 45–49.

351
Frueh, Terry; McGhee, Paul E.
Traditional sex-role development and amount of time spent watching television.
In: Developmental Psychology, 11/1975/1, pp. 109.

352
Leifer, Aimée Dorr; Lesser, Gerald S.
The development of career awareness in young children.
Cambridge, Mass.: Harvard Univ., Center for Research in Children's Television
1976. 72 pp.
(Arlington, Va.: ERIC ED 121 299)

353
McGhee, Paul E.
Television as a source of learning sex role stereotypes. Paper presented in a symposium on 'Environmental aspects of sex role behavior: Studies behind the nuclear family' at the meeting of the Society for Research in Child Development, Denver, Col., April 10–13, 1975.
n. p.: n. pr. 1975. 15 pp.
(Arlington, Va.: ERIC ED 111 528)

354
Miller, M. Mark; Reeves, Byron
Dramatic TV content and children's sex-role stereotypes.
In: Journal of Broadcasting, 20/1976/1, pp. 35–50.

355
Nicholas, Karen B.; McCarter, Robert E.; Heckel, Robert V.
The effects of race and sex on the imitation of television models.
In: Journal of Social Psychology, 85/1971/2, pp. 315–316.

356
Nicholas, Karen B.; McCarter, Robert E.; Heckel, Robert V.
Imitation of adult and peer television models by white and negro children.
In: Journal of Social Psychology, 85/1971/2, pp. 317–318.

357
Perry, David G.; Perry, Louise C.
Observational learning in children. Effects of sex of model and subject's sex role behavior.
In: Journal of Personality and Social Psychology, 31/1975/6, pp. 1083–1088.

358
Plost, Myrna; Rosen, Marvin J.
Effect of sex of career models on occupational preferences of adolescents.
In: AV Communication Review, 22/1974/1, pp. 41–50.

6.3 Political socialization

6.3.1 Literature reviews

360
Atkin, Charles K.
Communication and political socialization.
In: Political Communication Review, 2/1975/–, pp. 2–7.

361
Becker, Lee B.; McCombs, Maxwell E.; McLeod, Jack M.
The development of political cognitions.
In: Political Communication.
    Chaffee, Steven H. (Ed.)
    Beverly Hills, Ca.: Sage 1975, pp. 21–63.

362
Kraus, Sidney
Mass communication and political socialization. A re-assessment of two decades of research.
In: Quarterly Journal of Speech, 59/1973/4, pp. 390–400.

6.3.2 Surveys and experiments

363
Atkin, Charles K.; Greenberg, Bradley S.
Public television and political socialization. A field experiment on the impact of a public television series on the political knowledge, attitudes, and communication behaviors of adolescents. Final report.

Washington, D. C.: Corporation for Public Broadcasting 1974. 85 pp.
(Arlington, Va.: ERIC ED 121 259)

364
Atkin, Charles K.; Galloway, John; Nayman, Oguz B.
News media exposure, political knowledge and campaign interest.
In: Journalism Quarterly, 53/1976/2, pp. 231–237.

365
Atkin, Charles K.; Galloway, John; Nayman, Oguz B.
Reciprocal causality among political interest, political knowledge and mass
media exposure. Paper presented at the Annual Meeting of the International
Communication Association, New Orleans, April 17–20, 1974.
n. p.: n. pr. 1974. 23 pp.
(Arlington, Va.: ERIC ED 097 750)

366
Blumler, Jay G.; MacQuail, Denis; Nossiter, T. J.
Political communication and the young voter. A panel study, 1970–1971,
examining the role of election communication in the political socialisation
of first-time voters.
Social Science Research Council, London (Ed.)
n. p.: n. pr. 1975. 205 pp.

367
Blumler, Jay G.; MacQuail, Denis; Nossiter, T. J.
Political communication and the young voter in the general election of February
1974. A panel study, 1970–1974, examining influences on the political socialisation of young voters between their first and second election campaigns.
Social Science Research Council, London (Ed.)
n. p.: n. pr. 1976. 99 pp.

368
Chaffee, Steven H.; McLeod, Jack M.; Wackman, Daniel B.
Family communication patterns and adolescent political participation.
In: Socialization to politics. A reader.
    Dennis, Jack (Ed.)
    New York, N. Y.: Wiley 1973, pp. 349–364.

369
Chaffee, Steven H.; Ward, Scott L.; Tipton, Leonard P.
Mass communication and political socialization.
In: Journalism Quarterly, 47/1970/4, pp. 647–659.

German translation:
Chaffee, Steve H.; Ward, Scott L.; Tipton, Leonard P.
Massenkommunikation und politische Sozialisation.
In: Gesellschaftliche Kommunikation und Information, 2.
   Aufermann, Jörg (Ed.) et al.
   Frankfurt, M.: Athenäum Fischer Taschenb.-Verl. 1973, pp. 471–494.

370
Conway, Margaret; Stevens, A. Jay; Smith, Robert G.
The relation between media use and children's civic awareness.
In: Journalism Quarterly, 52/1975/3, pp. 531–538.

371
Dominick, Joseph R.
Television and political socialization.
In: Educational Broadcasting Review, 6/1972/1, pp. 48–56.

372
Eyre-Brook, Elizabeth
The role of the mass media in the political socialization of English adolescents.
In: Der Anteil der Massenmedien bei der Herausbildung des Bewußtseins in der
   sich wandelnden Welt.
   Konferenzprotokoll I.
   Sektion Journalistik, Karl-Marx-Univ. (Ed.)
   Leipzig: Sektion Journalistik, Karl-Marx-Univ. 1974, pp. 243–251.

373
Hartmann, Paul; Husband, Charles
The mass media and racial conflict.
In: Race, 12/1971/3, pp. 267–282.
   Also in:
   Sociology of mass communications. Selected readings.
   McQuail, Denis (Ed.)
   Harmondsworth: Penguin Books 1972, pp. 435–455.
   Also in:
   The manufacture of news. Social problems, deviance, and the mass media.
   Cohen, Stanley (Ed.); Young, Jock (Ed.)
   London: Constable 1974, pp. 270–283.

374
Hartmann, Paul; Husband, Charles
Racism and the mass media. A study of the role of the mass media in the
formation of white beliefs and attitudes in Britain.
London: Davis-Poynter 1974. 279 pp.

375
Hawkins, Robert P.; Pingree, Suzanne; Roberts, Donald F.
Watergate and political socialization.
In: American Politics Quarterly, 3/1975/4, pp. 406–422.

376
Hollander, Neil
Adolescents and the war. The sources of socialization.
In: Journalism Quarterly, 48/1971/3, pp. 472–479.

377
Home-school differences in political learning. Television's impact upon school
schildren's perceptions of national needs. Final report.
Meadow, Robert G. (Coll.); Frank, Robert S. (Coll.); West, Gerald T. (Coll.);
Lavipour, Farid (Coll.)
Foreign Policy Research Institute, Philadelphia (Ed.)
Philadelphia, Pa.: Foreign Policy Research Institute 1974. IV, 106 pp.
(Arlington, Va.: ERIC ED 121 669)

378
Johnson, Norris R.
Television and politization. A test of competing models.
In: Journalism Quarterly, 50/1973/3, pp. 447–455.

379
Lewellen, James R.
Mass media and political participation.
In: Social Education, 40/1976/6, pp. 457–461.

380
McMartin, Pamela A.
A cross-lag test of Lerner's model of modernization.
In: Journalism Quarterly, 51/1974/1, pp. 120–121.

381
Roberts, Donald F.; Hawkins, Robert P.; Pingree, Suzanne
Do the mass media play a role in political socialization?
In: The Australian and New Zealand Journal of Sociology,
    11/1975/2, pp. 37–43.

382
Rubin, Alan M.
Television in children's political socialization.
In: Journal of Broadcasting, 20/1976/1, pp. 51–60.

383*
Tolley, Howard Jr.
Children and war. Political socialization to international conflict.
New York, N. Y.: Teachers College Press, Columbia Univ. 1973. 196 pp.

* Current numbers 384–466 have been omitted for editorial reasons.

7. STUDIES ON THE EFFECTS OF TELEVISION VIOLENCE ON SOCIAL BEHAVIOR

7.1 Literature reviews, theoretical considerations

467
Bandura, Albert
Aggression. A social learning analysis.
Englewood Cliffs, N. J.: Prentice-Hall 1973. 390 pp.

468
Bandura, Albert; Walters, Richard H.
Der Erwerb aggressiver Verhaltensweisen durch soziales Lernen.
(The acquisition of aggressive behaviour through social learning.)
In: Aggressives Verhalten. Neue Ergebnisse der psychologischen Forschung.
    Schmidt-Mummendey, Amélie (Ed.) et al.
    München: Juventa 1972, pp. 107–129.

469
Bauer, Jutta; Bauer Erich
Weiterführende Aspekte zum Problem Fernsehen und aggressives Verhalten bei Kindern und Jugendlichen.
(Second thoughts on the problem of television and aggressive behaviour of children and young people.)
Stuttgart: Kohlhammer 1974. 144 pp.

470
Berkowitz, Leonard
Some determinants of impulsive aggression. Role of mediated associations with reinforcements for aggression.
In: Psychological Review, 81/1974/2, pp. 165–176.

471
Bessler, Hansjörg
Brutalität im Fernsehen.
(Brutality in television.)
In: Massenkommunikationsforschung. 2: Konsumtion.
    Prokop, Dieter (Ed.)
    Frankfurt a. M.: Fischer Taschenb.-Verl. 1973, pp. 253–274.

473
Brocher, Tobias
Gewaltdarstellungen im Fernsehen – Ventilfunktion oder Freisetzung von Aggressivität?

(Violence in television – safety valve or release of aggression?)
In: Fernsehen und Bildung, 5/1971/3–4, pp. 149–156.

474
Chaffee, Steven H.
Television and adolescent aggressivenes. Overview.
In: Television and social behavior. Reports and papers.
   Vol. III: Television and adolescent aggressiveness.
   Comstock, George A. (Ed.) et al.
   Washington, D. C.: U. S. Government Printing Office 1972, pp. 1–34.

475
Comstock, George
The evidence on television violence. Paper presented at National Homicide
Symposium, San Francisco, Oct., 1976.
Santa Monica, Calif.: Rand Corp. 1976. 14 pp.
(Arlington, Va.: ERIC ED 134 162)

476
Comstock, George
Types of portrayals and aggressive behavior. Effects of television.
In: Journal of Communication, 27/1977/3, pp. 189–198.

477
Crawford, Patricia; Matthews, Catherine; Campell, Patricia
The impact of violence on television on children. A review of literature.
North York, Board of Education (Ed.)
Willowdale, Ontario: North York, Board of Education 1976. 24 pp.
(Arlington, Va.: ERIC ED 127 975)

478
Dembo, Richard
The media and violence in society.
In: Internationale Zeitschrift für Kommunikationsforschung, 1/1974/3,
   pp. 420–442.

479
Dussich, John P. J.
Violence and the media.
In: Criminology, 8/1970/1, pp. 80–94.

480
Endsley, Richard C.; Osborn, D. Keith
Children's reactions to TV violence. A review of research.
In: Young Children, 26/1970/–, pp. 4–11.

481
Feshbach, Norma D.
The effects of violence in childhood.
In: Journal of Clinical Child Psychology, 2/1973/3, pp. 28–31.

482
Glucksmann, André
Violence on the screen. A report on research into the effects on young people
of scenes of violence in films and television.
London: British Film Institute Education Department 1971. 78 pp.

483
Goranson, Richard E.
Media violence and aggressive behavior. A review of experimental research.
In: Advances in experimental social psychology. Vol. 5.
    Berkowitz, L. (Ed.)
    New York: Academic Press 1970, pp. 1–31.

484
Greenberg, Bradley, S.
Televised violence. Further explorations.
In: Television and social behavior. Reports and papers.
    Vol. V: Television effects. Further explorations.
    Comstock, George A. (Ed.) et al.
    Washington, D. C.: U. S. Government Printing Office 1972, pp. 1–21.

485
Hoshino, K.
Mass communication and delinquency.
In: Journal of Educational Sociology, 25/1970/–, pp. 89–104.

486
Howitt, Dennis; Cumberbatch, Guy
Mass media violence and society.
London: Elek Science 1975. 167 pp.

487
Howitt, Dennis; Dembo, Richard
A subcultural account of media effects.
In: Human Relations, 27/1974/1, pp. 25–41.

488
Kaplan, Robert M.; Singer, Robert D.
Television violence and viewer aggression. A re-examination of the evidence.
In: Journal of Social Issues, 32/1976/4, pp. 35–70.

489
Kellner, Hella; Horn, Imme
Gewalt im Fernsehen. Ergebnisse bisheriger Wirkungsforschung.
(Violence in television – Results of effect research to date.)
In: Fernsehen und Bildung, 5/1971/3–4, pp. 141–148.

490
Kellner, Hella; Horn, Imme
Gewalt im Fernsehen. Literaturbericht über Medienwirkungsforschung.
(Violence in television. A review of literature on media effects research.)
Mainz: Zweites Deutsches Fernsehen 1971. 78 pp.

491
Kniveton, Bromley H.
Televised violence and the vulnerable child.
In: Proceedings of the Royal Society of Medicine, 66/1973/–, pp. 1135–1137.

492
Kniveton, Bromley H.
The very young and television violence.
In: Journal of Psychosomatic Research, 18/1974/4, pp. 233–237.

493
Koszyk, Kurt
Massenmedien und jugendliche Delinquenz.
(Mass media and juvenile delinquency.)
In: Publizistik, 16/1971/2, pp. 139–154.

494
Krebs, Dagmar
Wirkungen von Gewaltdarstellungen in Massenmedien – Katharsis oder
Stimulation?

(The effects of violence in the mass media – catharsis or stimulation?)
In: Zeitschrift für Sozialpsychologie, 4/1973/4, pp. 318–332.

495
Kunczik, Michael
Gewalt im Fernsehen. Eine Analyse der potentiell kriminogenen Effekte.
(Violence in television. An analysis of the potential crime-inducing effects.)
Köln: Böhlau 1975. 827 pp.

496
Lang, Gladys Engel; Lang, Kurt
Some pertinent questions on collective violence and the news media.
In: Journal of Social Issues, 28/1972/1, pp. 93–110.

497
Liebert, Robert M.
Television and children's aggressive behavior. Another look.
In: American Journal of Psychoanalysis, 34/1974/2, pp. 99–107.

498
Liebert, Robert M.
Television and social learning. Some relationships between viewing violence and
behaving aggressively. (Overview).
In: Television and social behavior. Reports and papers.
    Vol. II: Television and social learning.
    Murray, John P. (Ed.) et al.
    Washington, D. C.: U. S. Government Printing Office 1972, pp. 1–42.

499
Liebert, Robert M.
Television violence and children's aggression. The weight of the evidence.
In: Determinants and origins of aggressive behavior.
    DeWit, Jan (Ed.) et al.
    The Hague: Mouton 1974, pp. 525–532.

500
Lüscher, Kurt
Gewalt im Fernsehen – Gewalt des Fernsehens.
(Violence on television – violence of television.)
In: Aggressivität und Gewalt in unserer Gesellschaft.
    Neidthardt, Friedhelm (Coll.) et al.
    München: Juventa 1973, pp. 83–104.

501
Meyer, Timothy P.; Anderson, James A.
Media violence research. Interpreting the findings.
In: Journal of Broadcasting, 17/1973/4, pp. 447–458.

502
Murray, John P.
Television and children. Some problems in studying the impact of televised violence.
School of Behavioural Sciences, Macquarie Univ., Sydney (Ed.)
Sydney: Macquarie Univ., School of Behavioural Sciences 1976. 11 pp.

503
Popitz, Heinrich
Die Wirkung von Gewaltdarstellungen in Fernsehprogrammen.
(The effect of violence portrayals in television programs.)
In: Soziologische Studien, 5: Präsentation und Wirkung von Fernsehinhalten.
    Institut für Soziologie, Freiburg (Ed.)
    Freiburg: Institut für Soziologie 1972, pp. 1–13.

504
Schmidt-Mummendey, Amélie; Fröhlich, Werner
Aggressives Verhalten und Massenmedien. Probleme und experimentelle Ergebnisse.
(Aggressive behaviour and mass media. Problems and experimental results.)
In: Die Darstellung der Gewalt in den Massenmedien.
    Löffler, Martin (Ed.)
    München: Beck 1973, pp. 33–41.

505
Scott Andison, F.
TV violence and viewer aggression. A cumulation of study results 1956–1976.
In: Public Opinion Quarterly, 41/1977/3, pp. 314–331.

506
Selg, Herbert
Über Gewaltdarstellungen in Massenmedien. Eine psychologische Stellungnahme und Erwiderung auf den fernseheigenen Bericht zum Thema 'Gewalt im Fernsehen'.
(On the presentation of violence in mass media. A psychological commentary and reply to TV's own report on the subject 'violence in television'.)
In: Schriftenreihe der Bundesprüfstelle, –/1972/3, pp. 11–31.

507
Singer, Jerome L.
The influence of violence portrayed in television or motion pictures upon overt aggressive behavior.
In: The control of aggression and violence.
   Singer, Jerome L. (Ed.)
   New York: Academic Press 1971, pp. 19–60.

508
Stachiw, Alexander; Spiel, Georg
Entwicklung der Aggression bei Kindern. Eine Untersuchung am Beispiel des Fernsehens.
(The development of aggressiveness in children. Television as a case in point.)
München: Kindler 1976. 140 pp.

509
Strauss, Gloria D.; Poulos, Rita W.
A summary of the experimental effects of observing filmed aggression. TV and social learning: Appendix A.
In: Television and social learning. Reports and papers.
   Vol. II: Television and social learning.
   Murray, John P. (Ed.) et al.
   Washington, D. C.: U. S. Government Printing Office 1972, pp. 35–42.

510
Tannenbaum, Percy H.
Studies in film- and television-mediated arousal and aggression. A progress report.
In: Television and social behavior. Reports and papers.
   Vol. V: Television's effects. Further explorations.
   Rubinstein, Eli A. (Ed.) et al.
   Washington, D. C.: U. S. Government Printing Office 1972, pp. 309–350.

7.2 The research program of the Surgeon General's Scientific Advisory Committee on Television and Social Behavior

7.2.1 The reports

511
Television and growing up. The impact of televised violence.
Surgeon General's Scientific Advisory Committee on Television and Social

Behavior (Coll.); United States Dept. of Health, Education and Welfare (Ed.)
Washington, D. C.: U. S. Government Printing Office 1972. IX, 279 pp.
(Arlington, Va.: ERIC ED 057 595)

512
Television and social behavior. Reports and papers.
I. Media content and control.
A technical report to the Surgeon General's Scientific Advisory Committee on
Television and Social Behavior.
Comstock, George A. (Ed.); Rubinstein, Eli A. (Ed.)
United States Dept. of Health, Education, and Welfare (Ed.)
Washington, D. C.: U. S. Government Printing Office 1972. 546 pp.
(Arlington, Va.: ERIC ED 059 623)

513
Television and social behavior. Reports and papers.
II. Television and social learning.
A technical report to the Surgeon General's Scientific Advisory Committee on
Television and Social Behavior.
Murray, John P. (Ed.); Rubinstein, Eli A. (Ed.); Comstock, George A. (Ed.)
United States Dept. of Health, Education, and Welfare (Ed.)
Washington, D. C.: U. S. Government Printing Office 1972. 371 pp.
(Arlington, Va.: ERIC ED 059 624)

514
Television and social behavior. Reports and papers.
III. Television and adolescent aggressiveness.
A technical report to the Surgeon General's Scientific Advisory Committee on
Television and Social Behavior.
Comstock, George A. (Ed.); Rubinstein, Eli A. (Ed.)
United States Dept. of Health, Education, and Welfare (Ed.)
Washington, D. C.: U. S. Government Printing Office 1972. 435 pp.
(Arlington, Va.: ERIC ED 059 625)

515
Television and social behavior. Reports and papers.
IV. Television in day-to-day life. Patterns of use.
A technical report to the Surgeon General's Scientific Advisory Committee on
Television and Social Behavior.
Rubinstein, Eli A. (Ed.); Comstock, George A. (Ed.); Murray, John P. (Ed.)
United States Dept. of Health, Education, and Welfare (Ed.)
Washington, D. C.: U. S. Government Printing Office 1972. 603 pp.
(Arlington, Va.: ERIC ED 059 626)

516
Television and social behavior. Reports and papers.
V. Television's effects. Further explorations.
A technical report to the Surgeon General's Scientific Advisory Committee on
Television and Social Behavior.
Comstock, George A. (Ed.); Rubinstein, Eli A. (Ed.); Murray, John P. (Ed.)
United States Dept. of Health, Education, and Welfare (Ed.)
Washington, D. C.: U. S. Government Printing Office 1972. 375 pp.
(Arlington, Va.: ERIC ED 059 627)

7.2.2 Reviews and criticism

517
Atkin, Charles K.; Murray, John P.; Nayman, Oguz B.
The Surgeon General's research program on television and social behavior.
A review of empirical findings.
In: Journal of Broadcasting, 16/1971–72/1, pp. 21–35.

518
Bogart, Leo
Warning: The Surgeon General has determined that TV violence is moderately
dangerous to your child's mental health.
In: Public Opinion Quarterly, 36/1972–73/4, pp. 491–521.
German translation:
Bogart, Leo
Vorsicht: Es gibt Untersuchungen, die den Einfluß von Gewaltdarstellungen im
Fernsehen verharmlosen.
In: Rundfunk und Fernsehen, 22/1974/1, pp. 3–36.

519
Cater, Douglas; Strickland, Stephen
Communications and society. A first hard look at the Surgeon General's report
on television and violence.
Aspen Institute for Humanistic Studies, Palo Alto, Calif. (Ed.) Academy for
Educational Development, Washington, D. C. (Ed.)
Palo Alto, Calif: Aspen Program on Communications and Society 1972. 11 pp.
(Arlington, Va.: ERIC ED 081 175)

520
Cater, Douglas; Strickland, Stephen
TV violence and the child. The evolution and fate of the Surgeon General's report.
New York, N. Y.: Russell Sage Foundation 1975. 178 pp.

521
Comstock, George A.
Television violence: where the Surgeon General's study leads.
Santa Monica, Ca.: Rand 1972. 18 pp.

522
Hearings before the Subcommittee on Communications of the Committee on Commerce, United States Senate, 92nd Congress, 2nd session on the Surgeon General's report by the Scientific Advisory Committee on Television and Social Behavior.
United States Congress, Senate Committee on Commerce (Ed.)
Washington, D. C.: U. S. Government Printing Office 1972. V, 298 pp.
(Arlington, Va.: ERIC ED 063 761)

523
Murray, John P.
Television and violence. Implications of the Surgeon General's research program.
In: American Psychologist, 28/1973/6, pp. 472–478.
    Also in:
    Children and television.
    Brown, Ray (Ed.)
    London: Cassell and Collier Macmillan 1976, pp. 285–296.

524
Rubinstein, Eli A.
The TV violence report: what's next?
In: Journal of Cummunication, 24/1974/1, pp. 80–88.

525
Rubinstein, Eli A.
Warning: the Surgeon General's research program may be dangerous to preconceived notions.
In: Journal of Social Issues, 32/1976/4, pp. 18–34.

7.3 Relations between media use, program preferences and aggressive behavior (surveys, correlational studies)

526
Abel, John D.; Beninson, Maureen E.
Perceptions of TV program violence by children and mothers.
In: Journal of Broadcasting, 20/1976/3, pp. 355–363.

527
Becker, Gilbert
Causal analysis in R-R studies. Television violence and aggression.
In: American Psychologist, 27/1972/10, pp. 967–968.

528
Chaffee, Steven H.; McLeod, Jack M.
Adolescents, parents, and television violence. Paper presented at the symposium
"The early window. The role of television in childhood", American Psychological
Association Convention, Washington, D. C., September 1971.
n. p.: n. pr. 1971. 44 pp.
(Arlington, Va.: ERIC ED 054 641)

529
Chaney, David C.
Involvement, realism and the perception of aggression in television programmes.
In: Human Relations, 23/1970/5, pp. 373–381.

530
The convergence of laboratory and field studies of the development of aggression.
Eron, Leonard D. (Coll.); Walder, Leopold O. (Coll.); Huesman, L. Rowell
(Coll.); Lefkowitz, Monroe M. (Coll.)
In: Determinants and origins of aggressive behavior.
    DeWit, Jan (Ed.) et al.
    The Hague: Mouton 1974, pp. 348–380.

531
Does television violence cause aggression?
Eron, Leonard D. (Coll.); Lefkowitz, Monroe M. (Coll.); Huesman, L. Rowell
(Coll.); Walder, Leopold O. (Coll.)
In: American Psychologist, 27/1972/4, pp. 253–263.

532
Dominick, Joseph R.; Greenberg, Bradley S.
Attitudes toward violence. The interaction of television exposure, family
attitudes, and social class.
In: Television and social behavior. Reports and papers.
    Vol. III: Television and adolescent aggressiveness.
    Comstock, George A. (Ed.) et al.
    Washington, D. C.: U. S. Government Printing Office 1972, pp. 314–335.

533
Dominick, Joseph R.
Children's viewing of crime shows and attitudes on law enforcement.
In: Journalism Quarterly, 51/1974/1, pp. 5–12.

534
Donohue, Thomas R.
Black children's perceptions of favorite TV characters as models of antisocial behavior.
In: Journal of Broadcasting, 19/1975/2, pp. 153–168.

535
Friedman, Herbert L.; Johnson, Raymond L.
Mass media use and aggression. A pilot study.
In: Television and social behavior. Reports and papers,
   Vol. III: Television and adolescent aggressiveness.
   Comstock, George A. (Ed.) et al.
   Washington, D. C.: U. S. Government Printing Office 1972, pp. 336–360.

536
Greenberg, Bradley S.
British children and televised violence.
In: Public Opinion Quarterly, 38/1974–75/4, pp. 531–547.

537
Growing up to be violent. A longitudinal study of the development of aggression.
Lefkowitz, Monroe M. (Coll.); Eron, Leonard D. (Coll.); Walder, Leopold O. (Coll.); Huesman, L. Rowell (Coll.)
New York, N. Y.: Pergamon 1977. 236 pp.

538
Halloran, James D.; Brown, Roger, L.; Chaney, David C.
Television and delinquency.
Leicester: Leicester University Press 1970. 221 pp.

German translation:
Halloran, James D.; Brown, Roger L.; Chaney, David C.
Fernsehen und Kriminalität.
Berlin: Spiess 1972. 196 pp.

539
Havlik, Elisabeth; Zeug, Marianne; Spiel, Wolfgang
Untersuchung über mögliche Zusammenhänge zwischen Kriminalität und Fernsehen bei jugendlichen Rechtsbrechern.

(A study of the potential links between delinquency and television in the case of juvenile delinquents.)
In: Kriminalität, Brutalität und dargestellte Aggression im Fernsehen und ihre Wirkung auf die Öffentlichkeit.
Wien: Österreichischer Rundfunk 1974, pp. 157–229.

540
How learning conditions in early childhood – including mass media – relate to aggression in late adolescence. Paper presented at the Anniversary Meeting of the American Orthopsychiatry Association, 50th, New York, N. Y., May 30, 1973.
Eron, Leonard (Coll.); Huesman, L. Rowell (Coll.); Lefkowitz, Monroe M. (Coll.); Walder, Leopold O. (Coll.)
n. p.: n. pr. 1973. 17 pp.
(Arlington, Va.: ERIC ED 086 321)

541
Howitt, Dennis
Attitudes towards violence and mass media exposure.
In: Gazette, 18/1972/4, pp. 208–234.

542
Howitt, Dennis
Television and aggression. A counterargument.
In: American Psychologist, 27/1972/10, pp. 969–970.

543
Huesman, L. Rowell; Eron, Leonard; Walder, Leopold O.
Television violence and aggression. The causal effect remains.
In: American Psychologist, 28/1973/7, pp. 617–620.

544
Johnson, Raymond L.; Friedman, Herbert L.; Gross, Herbert S.
Four masculine styles in television programming. A study of the viewing preferences of adolescent males.
In: Television and social behavior. Reports and papers.
    Vol. III: Television and adolescent aggressiveness.
    Comstock, George A. (Ed.) et al.
    Washington, D. C.: U. S. Government Printing Office 1972, pp. 361–371.

545
Kaplan, Robert M.
On television as a cause of aggression.
In: American Psychologist, 27/1972/10, pp. 968–969.

546
Kay, Herbert
Weakness in the television-causes-aggression analysis by Eron et al.
In: American Psychologist, 27/1972/10, pp. 970–973.

547
Kenny, David A.
Threats to the internal validity of cross-lagged panel inference, as related to "Television violence and child aggression." A follow-up study.
In: Television and social behavior. Reports and papers.
    Vol. III: Television and adolescent aggressiveness.
    Comstock, George A. (Ed.) et al.
    Washington, D. C.: U. S. Government Printing Office 1972, pp. 136–140.

548
Korzenny, Felipe
The perceived reality of television and aggressive predispositions among children in Mexico. Paper presented at the Annual Meeting of the International Communication Association, Portland, Oregon, April 14–17, 1976.
n. p.: n. pr. 1976. 38 pp.
(Arlington, Va.: ERIC ED 122 336)

549
McIntyre, Jennie J.; Teevan, James J.; Hartnagel, Timothy
Television violence and deviant behavior.
In: Television and social behavior. Reports and papers.
    Vol. III: Television and adolescent aggressiveness.
    Comstock, George A. (Ed.) et al.
    Washington, D. C.: U. S. Government Printing Office 1972, pp. 383–435.

550
McLeod, Jack M.; Atkin, Charles K.; Chaffee, Steven H.
Adolescents, parents and television use. Adolescent self-report measures from Maryland and Wisconsin samples.
In: Television and social behavior. Reports and papers.
    Vol. III: Television and adolescent aggressiveness.
    Comstock, George A. (Ed.) et al.
    Washington, D. C.: U. S. Government Printing Office 1972, pp. 173–238.

551
McLeod, Jack M.; Atkin, Charles K.; Chaffee, Steven H.
Adolescents, parents, and television use: selfreport and other-report measures from the Wisconsin sample.

In: Television and social behavior. Reports and papers.
Vol. III: Television and adolescent aggressiveness.
Comstock, George A. (Ed.) et al.
Washington, D. C.: U. S. Government Printing Office 1972, pp. 239–313.

552
Milavski, J. Ronald; Pekowsky, Berton
Exposure to TV "violence" and aggressive behavior in boys, examined as
progress. A status report of a longitudinal study. Expanded version of a paper
read at 1972 Annual Meeting of the American Sociological Association.
Coffin, Thomas E. (Coll.); Tuchman, Sam (Coll.)
New York, N. Y.: National Broadcasting Company, Dept. of Social Research
1973. 67 pp.

553
Murray, Randall L.; Cole, Richard R.; Fedler, Fred
Teenagers and TV violence. How they rate and view it.
In: Journalism Quarterly, 47/1970/2, pp. 247–255.

554
Neale, John M.
Comment on "Television violence and child aggression." A follow-up study.
In: Television and social behavior. Reports and papers.
Vol. III: Television and adolescent aggressiveness.
Comstock, George A. (Ed.) et al.
Washington, D. C.: U. S. Government Printing Office 1972, pp. 141–148.

555
Preference for televised contact sports as related to sex differences in aggression.
Lefkowitz, Monroe M. (Coll.); Walder, Leopold O. (Coll.); Eron, Leonard D.
(Coll.); Huesman, L. Rowell (Coll.)
In: Developmental Psychology, 9/1973/–, pp. 417–420.

556
Rarick, David L.; Townsend, J. E.; Boyd, D. A.
Adolescent perceptions of police. Actual and as depicted in TV drama.
In: Journalism Quarterly, 50/1973/3, pp. 438–446.

557
Relation of learning in childhood to psychopathology and aggression in young
adulthood.
Eron, Leonard D. (Coll.); Lefkowitz, Monroe M. (Coll.); Walder, Leopold O.
(Coll.); Huesman, L. Rowell (Coll.)

In: Child personality and psychopathology. Current topics.
Vol. 1.
Davids, Anthony (Ed.)
New York, N. Y.: Wiley 1974, pp. 53–88.

558
Robinson, John P.; Bachman, Jerald G.
Television viewing habits and aggression.
In: Television and social behavior. Reports and papers.
   Vol. III: Television and adolescent aggressiveness.
   Comstock, George A. (Ed.) et al.
Washington, D. C.: U. S. Government Printing Office 1972, pp. 327–382.

559
Snow, Robert P.
How children interpret TV violence in play context.
In: Journalism Quarterly, 51/1974/1, pp. 13–21.

560
Teevan, James T. Jr.; Hartnagel, Timothy F.
The effect of television violence on the perceptions of crime by adolescents.
In: Sociology and Social Research, 60/1976/3, pp. 337–348.

561
Television violence and child aggression. A follow-up study.
Lefkowitz, Monroe M. (Coll.); Eron, Leonard D. (Coll.); Walder, Leopold O.
(Coll.); Huesman, L. Rowell (Coll.)
In: Television and social behavior. Reports and papers.
   Vol. III: Television and adolescent aggressiveness.
   Comstock, George A. (Ed.) et al.
Washington, D. C.: U. S. Government Printing Office 1972, pp. 35–135.

562
Violence and behavior disorders. The effects of television on children and
adolescents.
McCarthy, Elizabeth (Coll.); Langner, Thomas S. (Coll.); Gersten, Joanne C.
(Coll.) et al.
In: Journal of Communication, 25/1975/4, pp. 71–85.

563
Watt, James H.; Krull, Robert
An examination of three models of television viewing and aggression.
In: Human Communication Research, 3/1977/2, pp. 99–112.

7.4 Effect studies under experimental conditions

7.4.1 Comparisons of various age groups, developmental studies

564
Collins, W. Andrew
Aspects of television content and children's social behavior.
Westby, Sally Driscoll (Coll.); Gecy, Suzanne K. (Coll.); Keniston, Allen (Coll.);
Zimmermann, Stephen A. (Coll.)
Minneapolis, Minn.: Institute of Child Development, Univ. of Minnesota 1974.
var. pag. (138 pp.)
(Arlington, Va.: ERIC ED 114 302)

565
Collins, W. Andrew; Gecy, Suzanne K.
Children's responses to constructive and aggressive reactions to threat situations
in televised drama.
Minneapolis, Minn.: Institute of Child Development, Univ. of Minnesota 1974.
20 pp.
(Arlington, Va.: ERIC ED 114 313)

566
Collins, W. Andrew; Zimmermann, Stephen A.
Convergent and divergent social cues. Effects of televised aggression on children.
In: Communication Research, 2/1975/4, pp. 331–346.

567
Collins, W. Andrew
Effect of temporal separation between motivation, aggression, and consequences.
A developmental study.
In: Developmental Psychology, 8/1973/–, pp. 215–221.

568
Collins, W. Andrew; Berndt, Thomas J.; Hess, Valerie L.
Observational learning of motives and consequences for television aggression:
A developmental study.
In: Child Development, 45/1974/–, pp. 799–802.

569
Feshbach, Seymour; Singer, Robert D.
Television and aggression. An experimental field study.
San Francisco, Ca.: Jossey-Bass 1971. 186 pp.

570
Feshbach, Seymour; Singer, Robert D.
Television and aggression. A reply to Liebert, Sobol and Davidson.
In: Television and social behavior. Reports and papers.
V. Television's effects. Further explorations.
Comstock, George A. (Ed.) et al.
Washington, D. C.: U. S. Government Printing Office 1972, pp. 359–366.

571
Feshbach, Seymour; Singer, Robert D.
Television and aggression. Some reactions to the Liebert, Sobol and Davidson review and response.
In: Television and social behavior. Reports and papers.
V. Television's effects. Further explorations.
Comstock, George A. (Ed.) et al.
Washington, D. C.: U. S. Government Printing Office 1972, pp. 373–375.

572
Five year ABC research project "Anti-social and pro-social effects of television on children." Summary.
Lieberman Research, Inc. (Coll.)
American Broadcasting Company, New York (Ed.)
New York, N. Y.: American Broadcasting Co. 1976. 40 pp., Appx.
(Arlington, Va.: ERIC ED 125 638)

573
Heller, Melvin S.; Polsky, Samuel
Five year review of research sponsored by the American Broadcasting Company. September 1970 through August 1975. Overview.
American Broadcasting Company, New York (Ed.)
New York, N. Y.: American Broadcasting Co. 1976. 69 pp.
(Arlington, Va.: ERIC ED 125 637)

574
Heller, Melvin S.; Polsky, Samuel
Studies in violence and television.
New York, N. Y.: American Broadcasting Company 1976. a–c, V, 503 pp.
(Arlington, Va.: ERIC ED 126 850)

575
Katzman, Natan I.
Violence and color television. What children of different ages learn.

In: Television and social behavior. Reports and papers.
    Vol. V: Television's effects. Further explorations.
    Comstock, George A. (Ed.) et al.
    Washington, D. C.: U. S. Government Printing Office 1972, pp. 253–308.

576
Leifer, Aimée Dorr; Roberts, Donald F.
Children's responses to television violence.
In: Television and social behavior. Reports and papers.
    Vol. II: Television and social learning.
    Murray, John P. (Ed.) et al.
    Washington, D. C.: U. S. Government Printing Office 1972, pp. 43–180.

577
Liebert, Robert M.; Sobol, Michael D.; Davidson, Emily S.
Catharsis of aggression among institutionalized boys. Fact or artifact?
In: Television and social behavior. Reports and papers.
    V. Television's effects. Further explorations.
    Comstock, George A. (Ed.) et al.
    Washington, D. C.: U. S. Government Printing Office 1972, pp. 351–359.

578
Liebert, Robert M.; Davidson, Emily S.; Sobol, Michael P.
Catharsis of aggression among institutionalized boys. Further comments.
In: Television and social behavior. Reports and papers.
    V. Television's effects. Further explorations.
    Comstock, George A. (Ed.) et al.
    Washington, D. C.: U. S. Government Printing Office 1972, pp. 366–373.

579
Liebert, Robert M.; Baron, Robert A.
Effects of symbolic modeling on children's interpersonal aggression. Paper
presented at the Meeting of the Society for Research in Child Development.
Minneapolis, Minn., April 1971.
n. p.: n. pr. 1971. 26 pp.
(Arlington, Va.: ERIC ED 054 852)

580
Liebert, Robert M.; Baron, Robert A.
Short-term effects of televised aggression on children's aggressive behavior.
In: Television and social behavior. Reports and papers.
    Vol. II: Television and social learning.

Murray, John P. (Ed.) et al.
Washington, D. C.: U. S. Government Printing Office 1972, pp. 181–201.

581
Liebert, Robert M.; Baron, Robert A.
Some immediate effects of televised violence on children's behavior.
In: Developmental Psychology, 6/1973/3, pp. 469–475.

582
Thomas, Sally A.
Violent content in television. The effect of cognitive style and age in mediating
children's aggressive responses.
In: Proceedings of the Annual Convention of the American Psychological
    Association, Vol. 7 (1972), Part 1.
    Washington, D. C.: American Psychological Ass. 1972, pp. 97–98.

583
Wolf, Thomas M.
A developmental investigation of televised modeled verbalisations on resistance
to deviation.
In: Developmental Psychology, 6/1972/3, pp. 537.

584
Wotring, C. Edward; Greenberg, Bradley S.
Experiments in televised violence and verbal aggression: two exploratory studies.
In: Journal of Communication, 23/1973/4, pp. 446–460.

7.4.2 Preschool children

585
Cameron, Paul; Janky, Christine
The effects of TV violence upon children. A naturalistic experiment.
In: Proceedings of the Annual Convention of the American Psychological
    Association, Vol. 6 (1971), Part 1.
    Washington, D. C.: American Psychological Ass. 1971, pp. 233–234.

586
Cameron, Paul; Janky, Christine
The effects of viewing "violent" TV upon children's at-home and in-school
behavior.
n. p.: n. pr. 1971. 43 pp.
(Arlington, Va.: ERIC ED 057 388)

587
Drabman, Ronald S.; Thomas, Margaret H.
Children's imitation of aggressive and prosocial behavior when viewing alone and in pairs. Effects of television.
In: Journal of Communication, 27/1977/3, pp. 199–205.

588
Facial expressions of emotions while watching televised violence as predictors of subsequent aggression.
Ekman, Paul (Coll.); Liebert, Robert M. (Coll.); Friesen, Wallace V. (Coll.); Harrison, Randall (Coll.) et al.
In: Television and social behavior. Reports and papers.
  Vol. V: Television's effects. Further explorations.
  Comstock, George A. (Ed.) et al.
  Washington, D. C.: U. S. Government Printing Office 1972, pp. 22–58.

589
Friedrich, Lynette K.; Stein, Aletha H.
Aggressive and prosocial television programs and the natural behavior of preschool children.
Society for Research in Child Development: Monographs. Serial No. 151, Vol. 38, No. 4.
Chicago, Ill.: Univ. of Chicago Press 1973. 64 pp.

590
Influence upon imitative aggression of an imitating peer.
O'Carroll, Marianne (Coll.); O'Neal, Edgar (Coll.); McDonald, Peter (Coll.) et al.
In: Journal of Social Psychology, 101/1977/–, pp. 313–314.

591
Kniveton, Bromley H.; Stephenson, Geoffrey M.
The effect of pre-experience on imitation of an aggressive film model.
In: Journal of Social and Clinical Psychology, 9/1970/–, pp. 31–36.

592
Kniveton, Bromley H.
The effect of rehearsal delay on long-term imitation in filmed aggression.
In: British Journal of Psychology, 64/1973/2, pp. 259–265.

593
Kniveton, Bromley H.; Stephenson, Geoffrey M.
An examination of individual susceptibility to the influence of aggressive film models.
In: British Journal of Psychiatry, 122/1973/–, pp. 53–56.

594
Kniveton, Bromley H.
Social class and imitation of aggressive adult and peer models.
In: Journal of Social Psychology, 89/1973/–, pp. 311–312.

595
Linné, Olga
Reactions of children to violence on TV.
Sveriges Radio, Audience and Programme Research Department (Ed.)
Stockholm: Sveriges Radio 1971. 58 pp.
(Arlington, Va.: ERIC ED 054 632)

596
Osborn, D. Keith; Endsley, Richard C.
Emotional reactions of young children to TV violence.
In: Child Development, 42/1971/–, pp. 321–331.

597
Parton, David A.; Geshuri, Yossef
Learning of aggression as a function of presence of a human model, reponse intensity, and target of the response.
In: Journal of Experimental Child Psychology, 11/1971/–, pp. 491–504.

598
Rop, Ilse; Bauernstätter, Eva
Die Wirkung unterschiedlich aggressiver Fernsehfilme auf Kinder im Vorschul-alter.
(The effects of TV films of different degrees of aggressiveness on pre-school children.)
Österreichischer Rundfunk, Wien (Ed.)
In: Kriminalität, Brutalität und dargestellte Aggression im Fernsehen und ihre
    Wirkung auf die Öffentlichkeit.
    Wien: Österreichischer Rundfunk 1974, pp. 269–334.

599
Ross, Lee B.
The effects of viewed aggression on the group play of children. Paper presented at Midwestern Psychological Association Meeting, May 4–6, 1972, Cleveland, Ohio.
n. p.: n. pr. 1972. 25 pp.
(Arlington, Va.: ERIC ED 064 642)

600
Stein, Aletha H.; Friedrich, Lynette K.
Television content and young children's behavior.
Vondracek, Fred (Coll.)
In: Television and social behavior. Reports and papers.
    Vol. II: Television and social learning.
    Murray, John P. (Ed.) et al.
    Washington, D. C.: U. S. Government Printing Office 1972, pp. 202–317.

601
Steuer, Faye B.; Applefield, James M.; Smith, Rodney
Televised aggression and the interpersonal aggression of preschool children.
In: Journal of Experimental Child Psychology, 11/1971/–, pp. 442–447.

7.4.3 School children

602
Atkin, Charles K.; Wood, Charles
Effects of realistic vs. fictional television violence on aggression.
Paper presented at the Annual Meeting of the Association for Education in Journalism, College Park, Md., Aug. 1976.
n. p.: n. pr. 1976. 30 pp.
(Arlington, Va.: ERIC ED 124 979)

603
Auswirkungen von Verhaltensmodellen aus einem Fernsehwestern auf Gruppenarbeitsverhalten und Aggressionsbereitschaft von Grundschülern.
(The effects of models of behaviour from a TV western on group working behavior and aggressiveness of primary school children.)
Charlton, Michael (Coll.); Liebelt, Elsa (Coll.); Sültz, Jutta (Coll.);
Tausch, Anne-Marie (Coll.)
In: Psychologie in Erziehung und Unterricht, 21/1974/3, pp. 164–175.

604
Baran, Stanley J.
Prosocial and antisocial television content and modeling by high and low
self-esteem children.
In: Journal of Broadcasting, 18/1974/4, pp. 481–495.

605
Biblow, Ephraim
Imaginative play and the control of aggressive behavior.
In: Singer, Jerome L.
   The child's world of make-believe.
   New York, N. Y.: Academic Press 1973, pp. 104–128.

606
Children's violence perception as a function of TV violence.
Rabinovitch, Martin S. (Coll.); MacLean, Malcolm S. (Coll.); Markham, James
W. (Coll.); Talbot, Albert D. (Coll.)
In: Television and social behavior. Reports and papers.
   Vol. V: Television's effects. Further explorations.
   Comstock, George A. (Ed.) et al.
   Washington, D. C.: U. S. Government Printing Office 1972, pp. 231–252.

607
Cline, Victor B.; Croft, Roger G.; Courrier, Steven
Desensitization of children to television violence.
In: Journal of Personality and Social Psychology, 27/1973/3, pp. 360–365.

608
Drabman, Ronald S.; Thomas, Margaret H.
Does media violence increase children's toleration of real-life aggression?
In: Developmental Psychology, 10/1974/3, pp. 418–421.

609
Drabman, Ronald S.; Thomas, Margaret H.
Does TV violence breed indifference? The effects of television on children and
adolescents.
In: Journal of Communication, 25/1975/4, pp. 86–89.

610
Drabman, Ronald S.; Thomas, Margaret H.
Exposure to filmed violence and children's tolerance of real life aggression.
Paper presented at the Annual Meeting of the American Psychological

Association, 82nd, New Orleans, Louisiana, August 30–September 3, 1974.
n. p.: n. pr. 1974. 3 pp.
(Arlington, Va.: ERIC ED 097 075)

611
Effect of model-reward on the observer's recall of the modeled behavior.
Thelen, Mark H. (Coll.); McGuire, Dennis (Coll.); Simmonds, David W.
(Coll.); Akamatsu, T. John (Coll.)
In: Journal of Personality and Social Psychology, 29/1974/1, pp. 140–144.

612
Ellis, Glenn Thomas; Sekyra, Francis
The effects of aggressive cartoons on the behavior of first grade children.
In: Journal of Psychology, 81/1972/–, pp. 37–43.

613
Feshbach, Seymour
Reality and fantasy in filmed violence.
In: Television and social behavior. Reports and papers.
    Vol. II: Television and social learning.
    Murray, John P. (Ed.) et al.
    Washington, D. C.: U. S. Government Printing Office 1972, pp. 318–345.

614
Feshbach, Seymour
The role of fantasy in the response to television.
In: Journal of Social Issues, 32/1976/4, pp. 71–85.

615
Foulkes, David; Belvedere, Edward; Brubaker, Terry
Televised violence and dream content.
In: Television and social behavior. Reports and papers.
    Vol. V: Television's effects. Further explorations.
    Comstock, George A. (Ed.) et al.
    Washington, D. C.: U. S. Government Printing Office 1972, pp. 59–119.

616
Gordon, Thomas F.
The effects of time context on children's perceptions of aggressive television content.
Philadelphia, Pa.: Temple Univ., 1973. 24 pp.
(Arlington, Va.: ERIC ED 075 877)

617
Greenberg, Bradley S.; Gordon, Thomas F.
Social class and racial differences in children's perceptions of television violence.
In: Television and social behavior. Reports and papers.
   Vol. V: Television's effects. Further explorations.
   Comstock, George A. (Ed.) et al.
   Washington, D. C.: U. S. Government Printing Office 1972, pp. 185–210.

618
Hanratty, Margaret A.; O'Neal, Edgar; Sulzer, Jefferson L.
Effect of frustration upon imitation of aggression.
In: Journal of Personality and Social Psychology, 21/1972/1, pp. 30–34.

619
Hapkiewicz, Walter G.; Roden, Aubrey H.
The effect of aggressive cartoons on children's interpersonal play.
In: Child Development, 42/1971/5, pp. 1583–1585.

620
Hapkiewicz, Walter G.; Stone, Robert D.
The effect of realistic versus imaginary aggressive models on children's interpersonal play.
In: Child Study Journal, 4/1974/2, pp. 47–58.

621
Haynes, Richard B.
Children's perceptions of 'comic' and 'authentic' cartoon violence.
In: Journal of Broadcasting, 22/1978/1, pp. 63–70.

622
Kellner, Hella
Television as a socializing factor. Initial results of a study concerning the effects of television violence on viewers' behavior.
In: EBU Review, 27/1976/6, pp. 16–21.

623
Kellner, Hella
Television as a socialization factor. Interim results of a study concerning the effects of television violence on viewers' behavior.
In: EBU Review, 29/1978/2, pp. 13–16.

624
Lerner, Laurie; Weiss, Robert L.
Role of value of reward and model affective response in vicarious reinforcement.
In: Journal of Personality and Social Psychology, 21/1972/1, pp. 93–100.

625
Meyer, Timothy P.
Children's perceptions of justified/unjustified and fictional/real film violence.
In: Journal of Broadcasting, 17/1973/3, pp. 321–332.

626
Noble, Grant
Effects of different forms of filmed aggression on children's constructive and destructive play.
In: Journal of Personality and Social Psychology, 26/1973/1, pp. 54–59.

627
Noble, Grant
Film-mediated aggressive and creative play.
In: British Journal of Social and Clinical Psychology, 9/1970/1, pp. 1–7.

628
Rabinovitch, Martin S.
Violence perception as a function of entertainment value and TV violence.
In: Psychonomic Science, 29/1972/6 A, pp. 360–362.

629
Role of frustration and anger in the imitation of filmed aggression against a human victim.
Savitsky, Jeffrey C. (Coll.); Rogers, Ronald W. (Coll.); Izard, Carroll E. (Coll.); Liebert, Robert M. (Coll.)
In: Psychological Reports, 29/1971/–, pp. 807–810.

630
Thomas, Sally A.
The role of cognitive style variables in mediating the influence of aggressive television upon elementary school children.
n. p.: n. pr. 1972. 73 pp.
(Arlington, Va.: ERIC ED 065 175)

631
Wolf, Thomas M.
Effects of televised modeled verbalizations and behavior on resistance
to deviation.
In: Developmental Psychology, 8/1973/1, pp. 51–56.

632
Wolf, Thomas M.; Cheyne, J. Allan
Persistence of effects of live behavioral, televised behavioral, and live verbal
models on resistance to deviation.
In: Child Development, 43/1972/–, pp. 1429–1436.

7.4.4 Adolescents

633
Berkowitz, Leonard; Alioto, Joseph T.
The meaning of an observed event as an determinant of its aggressive consequences.
In: Journal of Personality and Social Psychology, 28/1973/2, pp. 206–217.

634
Clark, Cedric
Race, identification, and television violence.
In: Television and social behavior. Reports and papers.
    Vol. V: Television's effects. Further explorations.
    Comstock, George A. (Ed.) et al.
    Washington, D. C.: U. S. Government Printing Office 1972, pp. 120–184.

635
Cumberbatch, Guy; Howitt, Dennis
The effects of film hero identification on the moral values of adolescents.
Leicester: Centre for Mass Communication Research, Univ. of Leicester n. d.
(after 1972). 14 pp.

636
Cumberbatch, Guy; Howitt, Dennis
Identification with aggressive television characters and children's moral
judgments.
In: Determinants and origins of aggressive behavior.
    DeWit, Jan (Ed.) et al.
    The Hague: Mouton 1974. pp. 517–523.

637
Doob, Anthony N.; Climie, Robert J.
Delay of measurement and the effects of film violence.
In: Journal of Experimental Social Psychology, 8/1972/–, pp. 136–142.

638
Doob, Anthony N.; Kirshenbaum, Hershi M.
The effects on arousal of frustration and aggressive films.
In: Journal of Experimental Social Psychology, 9/1973/1, pp. 57–64.

639
Edgar, Patricia
Social and personality factors influencing learning from film and television.
Paper presented at the American Educational Research Association Annual
Conference, New Orleans, Louis., Feb. 25–March 1, 1973.
n. p.: n. pr. 1973. 25 pp.
(Arlington, Va.: ERIC ED 074 709)

640
Geen, Russell G.; Stonner, David; Kelley, David R.
Aggression anxiety and cognitive appraisal of aggression-threat stimuli.
In: Journal of Personality and Social Psychology, 29/1974/2, pp. 196–200.

641
Geen, Russell G.; Stonner, David
Context effects in observed violence.
In: Journal of Personality and Social Psychology, 25/1973/1, pp. 145–150.

642
Greenberg, Bradley S.; Gordon, Thomas F.
Children's perception of television violence. A replication.
In: Television and social behavior. Reports and papers.
    Vol. V: Television's effects. Further explorations.
    Comstock, George A. (Ed.) et al.
    Washington, D. C.: U. S. Government Printing Office 1972, pp. 211–230.

643
Guttmann, Giselher
Aggression, Kontext und Aktivierung. Der Sinnzusammenhang beobachteter
Aggressionen und die Aktivierung des Zuschauers als Determinanten medien-
abhängiger Verhaltensänderung.
(Aggression, context and activation. The interrelation of observed aggression and
the activation of the viewer as determinants of media-dependent behavioral
changes.)

Herkner, Werner (Coll.); Maderthaner, Rainer (Coll.); Sixt, Gerlinde (Coll.);
Vitouch, Peter (Coll.)
Österreichischer Rundfunk, Wien (Ed.)
In: Kriminalität, Brutalität und dargestellte Aggression im Fernsehen und ihre
    Wirkung auf die Öffentlichkeit.
    Wien: Österreichischer Rundfunk 1974, pp. 233–247.

644
Habituation and sensitization to filmed violence. Paper presented at the Mid-
western Psychological Association, Chicago, Ill., May 6–8, 1976.
Gange, J. J. (Coll.); Gabrenya, W. K. Jr. (Coll.); Geer, R. G. (Coll.); Quanty,
M. B. (Coll.)
n. p.: n. pr. 1976. 13 pp.
(Arlington, Va.: ERIC ED 134 890)

645
Howitt, Dennis; Cumberbatch, Guy
Affective feeling for a film character and evaluation of an anti-social act.
In: British Journal of Social and Clinical Psychology, 11/1972/–, pp. 102–108.

646
Hoyt, James L.
Effect of media violence "justification" on aggression.
In: Journal of Broadcasting, 14/1970/4, pp. 455–464.

647
Kelmer, Otto; Stein, Arnd
Fernsehen: Aggressionsschule der Nation? Die Entlarvung eines Mythos.
(Television: the nation's school of aggression? The exposure of a myth.)
Bochum: Brockmeyer 1975. 220 pp.

648
Krisch, Karl
Die Brutalität und Spannung von Filmszenen sowie die Aggressivität der
Zuschauer als Determinanten filminduzierter Aggressionen.
(Brutality and suspense of film scenes and the aggressiveness of viewers as
determinants of aggressions induced by films.)
Österreichischer Rundfunk, Wien (Ed.)
In: Kriminalität, Brutalität und dargestellte Aggression im Fernsehen und ihre
    Wirkung auf die Öffentlichkeit.
    Wien: Österreichischer Rundfunk 1974, pp. 251–266.

649
Leyens, Jacques-Philippe; Camino, Leoncio
The effects of repeated exposure to film violence on aggression and social structures.
In: Determinants and origins of aggressive behavior.
    DeWit, Jan (Ed.) et al.
    The Hague: Mouton 1975. pp. 509–516.

650
Menzies, Elisabeth S.
The effects of repeated exposure to televised violence upon attitudes towards violence among youthful offenders.
In: FCI Research Reports, 4/1972/–, pp. 1–43.

651
Meyer, Timothy P.
The effects of verbally violent film content on aggressive behavior.
In: Audiovisual Communication Review, 20/1972/2, pp. 160–169.

652
Meyer, Timothy P.
Effects of viewing justified and unjustified real film violence on aggressive behavior.
In: Journal of Personality and Social Psychology, 23/1972/1, pp. 21–29.

653
Milgram, Stanley; Shotland, R. Lance
Television and antisocial behavior. Field experiments.
New York, N. Y.: Academic Press 1973. 183 pp.

654
Noble, Grant
Discrimination between different forms of televised aggression by delinquent and non-delinquent boys.
In: British Journal of Criminology, 11/1970/3, pp. 230–244.

655
Noble, Grant
Some comments on the nature of delinquent's identification with television heroes, fathers and best friends.
In: British Journal of Social and Clinical Psychology, 10/1971/–, pp. 172–180.

656
Parke, Ross D.
A field experimental approach to children's aggression. Some methodological problems and some future trends.
In: Determinants and origins of aggressive behavior.
DeWit, Jan (Ed.) et al.
The Hague: Mouton 1974, pp. 500–508.

657
Schuch, Bibiana
Aggression im Film. Die Abhängigkeit der Beobachterreaktion von der Stärke des im Film dargebotenen aggressiven Verhaltens.
(Aggression in films. The dependency of observer reaction on the intensity of aggressive behavior presented in the film.)
Österreichischer Rundfunk, Wien (Ed.)
In: Kriminalität, Brutalität und dargestellte Aggression im Fernsehen und ihre Wirkung auf die Öffentlichkeit.
Wien: Österreichischer Rundfunk 1974, pp. 127–156.

658
Schwartz, Hans-Joachim; Eckert, Jochen; Bastine, Rainer
Die Wirkung eines aggressiven Films auf Jugendliche unter variierten Bedingungen.
(The effects of an aggressive film on young people under various conditions.)
In: Zeitschrift für Entwicklungspsychologie und pädagogische Psychologie, 3/1971/4, pp. 304–315.

659
Tannenbaum, Percy H.; Zillmann, Dolf
Emotional arousal in the facilitation of aggression through communication.
In: Advances in experimental social psychology, Vol. 8.
Berkowitz, Leonard (Ed.)
New York, N. Y.: Academic Press 1975, pp. 149–192.

660
Turner, Charles W.; Berkowitz, Leonard
Identifications with film aggressor (covert role taking) and reactions to film violence.
In: Journal of Personality and Social Psychology, 21/1972/2, pp. 256–264.

661
Wilkins, Judy L.; Scharff, William H.; Schlottmann, Robert S.
Personality type, reports of violence, and aggressive behavior.
In: Journal of Personality and Social Psychology, 30/1974/2, pp. 243–247.

662
Williams, Wenmouth Jr.; Wotring, C. Edward
Mediated violence and victim consequences. A behavioral measure of attention and interest.
In: Journal of Broadcasting, 20/1976/3, pp. 365–372.

663
Wotring, C. Edward; Greenberg, Bradley S.
Experiments in televised violence and verbal aggression. Two exploratory studies.
In: Journal of Communication, 23/1973/4, pp. 446–460.

664
Zillmann, Dolf
Excitation transfer in communication-mediated aggressive behavior.
In: Journal of Experimental Social Psychology 7/1971/–, pp. 419–434.

665
Zillmann, Dolf; Johnson, Rolland C.
Motivated aggressiveness perpetuated by exposure to aggressive films and reduced by exposure to non-aggressive films.
In: Journal of Research in Personality, 7/1973/–, pp. 261–276.

666
Zillmann, Dolf; Johnson, Rolland C.; Hanrahan, John
Pacifying effect of happy ending of communication involving aggression.
In: Psychological Reports, 32/1973/–, pp. 967–970.

667
Zillmann, Dolf; Hoyt, James L.; Day, Kenneth D.
Strength and duration of the effect of aggressive, violent, and erotic communications on subsequent aggressive behavior.
In: Communication Research, 1/1974/3, pp. 286–306.

8. STUDIES ON THE EFFECTS OF PROSOCIAL CONTENT

8.1 Literature reviews

668
Baran, Stanley J.
Television as teacher of prosocial behavior. What the research says.
In: Public Telecommunications Review, 2/1974/3, pp. 46–51.

669
Brown, J. Ray
Sozial wünschbare Wirkungen des Fernsehens – gibt es die? Ergebnisse sozial-wissenschaftlicher Forschung zu prosozialen Effekten des Fernsehens.
(Socially desirable effects of television – are there any? Findings of social science research on prosocial effects of television.)
In: Media Perspektiven, –/1977/11, pp. 625–635.

8.2 Surveys and experiments

670
Assessing television's influence on children's prosocial behavior.
Rubinstein, Eli A. (Coll.); Liebert, Robert M. (Coll.); Neale, John M. (Coll.); Poulos, Rita W. (Coll.)
Stony Brook, N. Y.: Brookdale International Institute 1974. 27 pp., 15 pp. Appx.

671
Bryan, James H.; Walbeck, Nancy H.
The impact of words and deeds concerning altruism upon children.
In: Child Development, 41/1970/–, pp. 747–757.

672
Cosgrove, Michael; McInyre, Curtis W.
The influence of 'Misterogers Neighborhood' on nursery school children's prosocial behavior. Paper presented at the Biennial Southeastern Conference of the Society for Research in Child Development, 3rd, Chapel Hill, North Carolina, March 1974.
n. p.: n. pr. 1974. 14 pp.
(Arlington, Va.: ERIC ED 097 974)

673
Friedrich, Lynette K.; Stein, Aletha, H.; Susman, Elizabeth
The effects of prosocial television and environmental conditions on preschool
children. Paper presented at the Annual Meeting of the American Psychological
Association, 83rd, Chicago, Ill., August 30–September 3, 1975.
n. p.: n. pr. 1975. 14 pp.
(Arlington, Va.: ERIC ED 119 815)

674
Friedrich, Lynette K.; Stein, Aletha H.
A naturalistic study of the effects of prosocial television and environmental
variables on the behavior of young children. Final report.
University Park, Pa.; Pennsylvania State University 1975. 126 pp.
(Arlington, Va.: ERIC ED 111 438)

675
Friedrich, Lynette K.; Stein, Aletha H.
Prosocial television and young children. The effects of verbal labeling and role
playing on learning and behavior.
In: Child Development, 46/1975/1, pp. 27–38.

676
Goldberg, Marvin E.; Gorn, Gerald J.
Television's impact. Changing children's attitudes in a prosocial direction.
n. p.: n. pr. 1974. 8 pp.
(Arlington, Va.: ERIC ED 119 818)

677
Leifer, Aimée Dorr
Encouraging social competence with television.
New York, N. Y.: Children's Television Workshop 1973. 35 pp.
(Arlington, Va.: ERIC ED 122 807)

678
Leifer, Aimée Dorr
How to encourage socially-valued behavior. Paper presented at the Biennial
Meeting of the Society for Research in Child Development, Denver, Col.; April
10–13, 1975.
n. p.: n. pr. 1975. 11 pp.
(Arlington, Va.: ERIC ED 114 175)

Eguchi, H. (Ed.) et al.
Tokyo: Nippon Hoso Kyokai 1975, pp. 63–86.

775
Yin, Robert K.
The workshop and the world. Toward an assessment of the Children's
Television Workshop.
Santa Monica, Ca.: Rand 1973. 51 pp.

776
Zehrfeld, Klaus
Die Zusammenarbeit von Wissenschaftlern und Fernsehproduzenten im
Children's Television Workshop.
(The cooperation between researchers and TV producers in Children's
Television Workshop.)
In: Fernsehen und Bildung, 10/1976/1–2, pp. 24–33.

9.2 'The Electric Company'

777
Ball, Samuel; Bogatz, Gerry Ann
Reading with television. An evaluation of the Electric Company.
Vol. 1.
Rubin, Donald B. (Coll.); Beaton, Albert E. (Coll.)
Princeton, N. J.: Educational Testing Service 1973. 187 pp., Appx.
(Arlington, Va.: ERIC ED 073 178)

778
Ball, Samuel; Bogatz, Gerry Ann
Reading with television. An evaluation of the Electric Company.
Vol. 2.
Rubin, Donald B. (Coll.); Beaton, Albert E. (Coll.)
Princeton, N. J.: Educational Testing Service 1973. n. pag.
(Arlington, Va.: ERIC ED 073 178)

779
Ball, Samuel; Bogatz, Gerry Ann
A summary of the major findings from "Reading with television. An evaluation
of the Electric Company".
Princeton, N. J.: Educational Testing Service 1973. 14 pp.

780
Cazden, Courtney B.
Watching children watch 'The Electric Company'. An observation study in ten classrooms.
New York, N. Y.: Children's Television Workshop 1974. 90 pp.
(Arlington, Va.: ERIC ED 126 861)

781
Chen, Milton
Verbal response to 'The Electric Company'. Qualities of program material and the viewing condition which affect verbalization.
New York, N. Y.: Children's Television Workshop 1972. 48 pp.
(Arlington, Va.: ERIC ED 126 862)

782
The Electric Company. Television and reading, 1971–1980.
A mid-experiment appraisal. Editorial backgrounder.
Cooney, Joan Ganz (Ed.); Children's Television Workshop, New York (Ed.)
New York: Children's Television Workshop 1976. 31 pp.

783
Five years of 'The Electric Company'. Television and reading 1971–1976.
Cooney, Joan Ganz (Ed.)
New York, N. Y.: Children's Television Workshop 1975. 28 pp.
(Arlington, Va.: ERIC ED 122 805)

784
Herriott, Robert E.; Liebert, Roland J.
'The Electric Company' in-school utilization study. The 1971–72 school and teacher surveys.
New York, N. Y.: Children's Television Workshop 1972. 164 pp.
(Arlington, Va.: ERIC ED 073 709)

785
Liebert, Roland J.
'The Electric Company' in-school utilization study.
Vol. 2: The 1972–73 school and teacher surveys and trends since fall 1971.
Center for the Study of Education, Tallahassee, Fla. (Ed.)
n. p.: n. pr. 1973. 238 pp.
(Arlington, Va.: ERIC ED 094 775)

786
Mock, Karen R.
Children's attention to television. The effects of audio-vusial attention factors on children's television viewing strategies. Paper presented at the Annual Meeting of the American Educational Research Association, San Francisco, Ca., April 19–23, 1976.
n. p.: n. pr. 1976. 12 pp.
(Arlington, Va.: ERIC ED 122 832)

787
O'Bryan, Kenneth G.
Cues and attention to the visual display in children's television.
New York, N. Y.: Children's Television Workshop n. d. (probably 1975). 12 pp.
(Arlington, Va.: ERIC ED 122 810)

788
O'Bryan, Kenneth G.; Silverman, Harry
Report on children's television viewing strategies.
New York, N. Y.: Children's Television Workshop 1972. 17 pp.
(Arlington, Va.: ERIC ED 126 871)

789
O'Bryan, Kenneth G.; Silverman, Harry
Research report. Experimental program eye movement study.
New York, N. Y.: Children's Television Workshop 1973. 10 pp.
(Arlington, Va.: ERIC ED 126 870)

790
Reading with television. A follow-up evaluation of the Electric Company.
Ball, Samuel (Coll.); Bogatz, Gerry Ann (Coll.); Kazarow, Kathryn M. (Coll.); Rubin, Donald B. (Coll.)
New York, N. Y.: Children's Television Workshop 1974. 122 pp., 110 pp. Appx.
(Arlington, Va.: ERIC ED 122 798)

791
Rust, Langbourne W.
Attributes of The Electric Company pilot shows that produced high and low visual attention in 2nd and 3rd graders.
New York, N. Y.: Children's Television Workshop 1971. 48 pp.
(Arlington, Va.: ERIC ED 126 872)

792
Rust, Langbourne W.
The Electric Company distractor data. The influence of context.
New York, N. Y.: Children's Television Workshop 1971. 9 pp.
(Arlington, Va.: ERIC ED 122 812)

793
Rust, Langbourne W.
Visual attention to material in 'The Electric Company'. Summary of attribute research.
New York, N. Y.: Children's Television Workshop 1974. 7 pp.
(Arlington, Va.: ERIC ED 122 813)

794
Sproull, Natalie L.; Ward, Eric F.; Ward, Marilyn D.
Reading behaviors of young children who viewed 'The Electric Company'.
A final report.
New York, N. Y.: Children's Television Workshop 1976. 174 pp.
(Arlington, Va.: ERIC ED 122 815)

9.3 'Around the Bend'

795
Bertram, Charles L.; Pena, Deagelia; Hines, Brainard W.
Evaluation report. Early childhood education program 1969–1970 field test.
Summary report.
Charleston, W. Va.: Div. of Research and Evaluation, Appalachia Educational Laboratory 1971. 26 pp.
(Arlington, Va.: ERIC ED 052 837)

796
Cagno, Dick; Shively, Joe E.
Children's reactions to segments of a children's television series.
Appalachia Educational Laboratory, Charleston, W. Va. (Ed.)
Charleston, W. Va.: Appalachia Educational Laboratory 1973. 27 pp.
(Arlington, Va.: ERIC ED 093 357)

797
Hines, Brainard W.
Analysis of visual perception of children in the Appalachia preschool education program.

Charleston, W. Va.: Appalachia Educational Laboratory 1971. 23 pp.
(Arlington, Va.: ERIC ED 062 019)

798
Hines, Brainard W.
Attainment of cognitive objectives.
Appalachia Educational Laboratory, Charleston, W. Va. (Ed.)
Charleston, W. Va.: Appalachia Educational Lab. 1971. 15 pp.
(Arlington, Va.: ERIC ED 062 017)

799
Hines, Brainard W.
Children's reactions to types of television.
Charleston, W. Va.: Appalachia Educational Laboratory 1973. 44 pp.
(Arlington, Va.: ERIC ED 093 353)

800
Miller, George L.
Analysis of children's reactions to AEL's preschool television program.
Appalachia Educational Laboratory, Charleston, Division of Research and
Evaluation (Ed.)
Charleston, W. Va.: Appalachia Educational Laboratory 1970. 7 pp.
(Arlington, Va.: ERIC ED 052 841)

801
Miller, George L.
Analyzing viewer reactions to a preschool television program.
In: Journal of Educational Research, 66/1972/4, pp. 150–152.

802
Miller, George L.
Measuring children's curiosity.
Charleston, W. Va.: Appalachia Educational Laboratory 1971. 9 pp.
(Arlington, Va.: ERIC ED 062 022)

803
Pena, Deagelia; Miller, George L.
Analysis of children's social skills development and their reactions to a
preschool television program.
Charleston, W. Va.: Appalachia Educational Lab. 1971. 29 pp.
(Arlington, Va.: ERIC ED 057 884)

9.4 'Carrascolendas'

804
Laosa, Luis M.
Carrascolendas. A formative evaluation.
Los Angeles, Ca.: University of California 1973. 44 pp., App. (160 leaves in var. pag.)
(Arlington, Va.: ERIC ED 090 968)

805
Laosa, Luis M.
Viewing bilingual multicultural educational television. An empirical analysis of children's behaviors during television viewing.
In: Journal of Educational Psychology, 68/1976/2, pp. 133–142.

806
Wart, Geraldine van
Carrascolendas. Evaluation of a Spanish-English educational television series within region XIII. Final report. Evaluation component.
Austin, Texas: Education Service Center Region XIII 1974. XIV, 228 pp.
(Arlington, Va.: ERIC ED 092 089)

807
Williams, Frederick; Wart, Geraldine van; Stanford, Monty
Carrascolendas. National evaluation of a Spanish-English educational television series. 3rd year evaluation. Final report.
Austin, Texas: Center for Communication Research, School of Communication, Univ. of Texas 1973. XXIV, 403 pp.
(Arlington, Va.: ERIC ED 078 679)

808
Williams, Frederick; Natalicio, Diana S.
Evaluating 'Carrascolendas'. A television series for Mexican-American children.
In: Journal of Broadcasting, 16/1972/3, pp. 299–309.

809
Williams, Frederick; Valenzuela, Nicholas A.; Knight, Pamela
Prediction of Mexican-American communication habits and attitudes.
Austin, Texas: Center for Communication Research, Univ. of Texas 1973. 25 pp.

9.5 Other series

810
Earth's a Big Blue Marble. A Report of the impact of a children's television series on children's opinions.
Roberts, Donald F. (Coll.); Herold, Cecile (Coll.); Hornby, Melinda (Coll.); King, Sue (Coll.) et al.
Stanford, Ca.: Stanford Univ., Institute for Communication Research 1974.
76 pp.
(Arlington, Va.: ERIC ED 119 627)

811
An evaluation report on Vegetable Soup. The effects of a multi-ethnic children's television series on intergroup attitudes of children. Precis and overview.
Mays, Luberta (Coll.); Henderson, Edward H. (Coll.); Seidmann, Sylvia K. (Coll.); Steiner, Veronka J. (Coll.)
n. p.: n. pr. 1975. 43 pp.
(Arlington, Va.: ERIC ED 120 204)

812
On meeting real people. An evaluation report on Vegetable Soup. The effects of multi-ethnic children's television series on intergroup attitudes of children. Final report.
Mays, Luberta (Coll.); Henderson, Edward H. (Coll.); Seidman, Sylvia K. (Coll.); Steiner, Veronka J. (Coll.)
n. p.: n. pr. 1975. XXI, 203 pp.
(Arlington, Va.: ERIC ED 123 319)

813
Pflüger, Ulrike; Wingert, Gerhard
Vorschulfernsehen. Untersuchung von Sendungen aus der Vorschulreihe ‚Das feuerrote Spielmobil'. Ergebnisbericht.
(Preschool television. A study of programs from the preschool series 'Das feuerrote Spielmobil'. Reports of results.)
Wissenschaftliches Institut für Jugend- und Bildungsfragen in Film und Fernsehen, München (Ed.)
München: Wissenschaftliches Institut für Jugend- und Bildungsfragen in Film und Fernsehen 1974. 66, 21 pp.

10. STUDIES ON THE EFFECTS OF NEWS AND INFORMATION PROGRAMS

814
Alper, S. William; Leidy, Thomas R.
The impact of information transmission through television.
In: Public Opinion Quarterly, 33/1970/4, pp. 556–562.

815
Atkin, Charles K.
Broadcast news programming and child audience.
In: Journal of Broadcasting, 22/1978/1, pp. 47–61.

816
Atkin, Charles K.; Gantz, Walter
Children's responses to broadcast news. Exposure, evaluation, and learning.
Paper presented at the Annual Meeting of the Association for Education in Journalism, San Diego, Ca., August 18–21, 1974.
n. p.: n. pr. 1974. 24 pp. Appx.
(Arlington, Va.: ERIC ED 097 707)

817
Atkin, Charles K.
Effect of campaign advertising and newscasts on children.
In: Journalism Quarterly, 54/1977/3, pp. 503–508.

818
Atkin, Charles K.; Gantz, Walter
How children use television news programming. Patterns of exposure and effects. Paper presented at the Annual Meeting of the Int. Communication Association, New Orleans, Louisiana, April 17–20, 1974.
n. p.: n. pr. 1974. 30 pp.
(Arlington, Va.: ERIC ED 094 431)

819
Cohen, Akiba A.; Harrison, Randall P.; Wigand, Rolf T.
Affect and learning in TV news viewing by children. Final report.
Michigan State University, East Lansing, Mich., Department of Communication (Ed.)
East Lansing, Mich.: Dept. of Communication, Michigan State Univ. 1974. 16 pp.

820
Cohen, Akiba A.; Wigand, Rolf T.; Harrison, Randall P.
The effects of emotion-arousing events on children's learning from TV news.
In: Journalism Quarterly, 53/1976/2, pp. 204–210.

821
Cohen, Akiba A.; Wigand, Rolf T.; Harrison, Randall P.
The effects of type of event, proximity and repetition on children's attention to and learning from television news.
In: Communications, 3/1977/1, pp. 30–46.

822
Cushing, William G.; Lemert, James B.
Has TV altered students' news media preferences?
In: Journalism Quarterly, 50/1973/–, pp. 138–141.

823
Friedlander, Bernard Z.; Wetstone, Harriet S.; Scott, Christopher S.
Suburban preschool children's comprehension of an age-appropriate informational television program.
In: Child Development, 45/1974/–, pp. 561–565.

824
Halloran, James D.; Eyre-Brook, Elizabeth
Children and television news.
Copenhagen: Danish Radio 1970. 126 pp.

825
Information programmes for children 7 to 12 years old.
Fifth EBU Workshop for producers and directors of television programmes for children, Remscheid, 4–11 April 1976.
Werner, Peter (Ed.); European Broadcasting Union (Ed.)
Geneva: EBU 1977. 58 pp.

826
Torney, Judith V.
The influence of current affairs broadcasting upon pupil attitudes toward politics.
In: Television and world affairs teaching in schools. Report of the 9th Atlantic
    study conference on education organized at Bordeaux by the Atlantic
    Information Centre for Teachers, 3–9 September, 1972.
    Eppstein, John (Ed.); Atlantic Information Centre for Teachers, London (Ed.)
    London: Atlantic Information Centre for Teachers n. d. (1972 or later),
    pp. 12–18.

11. STUDIES ON THE EFFECTS OF TELEVISION ADVERTISING

11.1 Literature reviews

827
Broadcast advertising and children. Hearings before the Subcommittee on
Communications of the Committee on Interstate and Foreign Commerce, House
of Representatives, 94th Congress, 1st session, July 14–17, 1975.
United States Congress, Committee on Interstate and Foreign Commerce (Ed.)
Washington, D. C.: U. S. Government Printing Office 1976. V, 495 pp.
(Arlington, Va.: ERIC ED 128 816)

828
Choate, Robert B.; Engle, Pamela C.
Edible TV. Your child and food commercials. Part 1. A compilation for
relevant testimony before the Federal Trade Commission. 1976–77.
Washington, D. C.: Council of Children, Media and Merchandising 1977. 70 pp.

829
Research on the effects of television advertising on children. A review of the
literature and recommendations for future research.
Adler, Richard P. (Coll.); Friedlander, Bernard Z. (Coll.); Lesser, Gerald S.
(Coll.); Meringoff, Laurene (Coll.) et al.
National Science Foundation, Washington, D. C. (Ed.)
Washington, D. C.: U. S. Government Printing Office, Superintendent of
Documents 1977. 230 pp.
(Arlington, Va.: ERIC ED 145 499)

830
Robertson, Thomas S.
The impact of television advertising on children.
In: Wharton Quarterly, 7/1972/1, pp. 38–41.

831
Sheikh, Anees A.; Prasad, V. Kanti; Rao, Taaniru R.
Children's TV commercials: A review of research.
In: Journal of Communication, 24/1974/4, pp. 126–136.

832
Ward, Scott
Consumer socialization.
In: Journal of Consumer Research, 1/1974/September, pp. 1–14.

833
Ward, Scott; Wackman, Daniel B.
Effects of television advertising on consumer socialization.
Faber, Ronald (Coll.); Lesser, Gerald S. (Coll.)
Marketing Science Institute (Ed.)
Cambridge, Mass.: Marketing Science Inst. 1975. 48 pp., 13 pp. Appx.

834
Ward, Scott
Effects of television advertising on children and adolescents.
In: Television and social behavior. Reports and papers.
    Vol. IV: Television in day-to-day life. Patterns of use.
    Rubinstein, Eli A. (Ed.) et al.
    Washington, D. C.: U. S. Government Printing Office 1972, pp. 432–451.
    Also in:
    Children and television.
    Brown, Ray (Ed.)
    London: Cassell and Collier Macmillan 1976, pp. 297–319.

835
Ward, Scott; Wackman, Daniel B.; Wartella, Ellen
How children learn to buy. The development of consumer information-processing skills.
Beverly Hills, Ca.: Sage 1977. 271 pp.

11.2 Surveys and experiments

836
Atkin, Charles K.
The effects of television advertising on children.
1. First year experimental evidence. Final report.
East Lansing, Mich.: State University, College of Communication Arts 1975.
110 pp.
(Arlington, Va.: ERIC ED 116 783)

837
Atkin, Charles K.
The effects of television advertising on children.
2. Second year experimental evidence. Final report.
East Lansing, Mich.: State University, College of Communication Arts 1975.
59 pp.
(Arlington, Va.: ERIC ED 116 784)

838
Atkin, Charles K.; Culley, James
The effects of television advertising on children.
4. Attitudes of industry executives, government officials and consumer critics
toward children's advertising. Final report.
East Lansing, Mich.: State University, College of Communication Arts 1975.
99 pp.
(Arlington, Va.: ERIC ED 116 786)

839
Atkin, Charles K.
The effects of television advertising on children.
5. Content analysis of children's television commercials. Final report.
East Lansing, Mich.: State University, College of Communication Arts 1975.
36 pp.
(Arlington, Va.: ERIC ED 116 787)

840
Atkin, Charles K.
The effects of television advertising on children.
6. Survey of pre-adolescent's responses to television commercials. Final report.
East Lansing, Mich.: State University, College of Communication Arts 1975.
136 pp.
(Arlington, Va.: ERIC ED 116 820)

841
Atkin, Charles K.
The effects of television advertising on children. Survey of children's and
mother's responses to television commercials. Final report.
East Lansing, Mich.: State University, College of Communication Arts (Ed.)
n. p.: n. pr. 1975. 108 pp.
(Arlington, Va.: ERIC ED 123 675)

842
Atkin, Charles K.
Television advertising and children's observational modeling. Paper presented
at the Annual Meeting of the International Communication Association, Portland,
Oregon, April 14–17, 1976.
n. p.: n. pr. 1976. 29 pp., 5 pp. Appx.
(Arlington, Va.: ERIC ED 122 331)

843
Baumer, Larry; Starkey, John
Attitudes of students in grades six, eight, and twelve toward television commercials.
n. p.: n. pr. 1973. 14 pp.
(Arlington, Va.: ERIC ED 077 233)

844
Blatt, Joan; Spencer, Lyle; Ward, Scott
A cognitive development study of children's reactions to television advertising.
In: Television and social behavior. Reports and papers.
   Vol. IV: Television in day-to-day life. Patterns of use.
   Rubinstein, Eli A. (Ed.) et al.
   Washington, D. C.: U. S. Government Printing Office 1972, pp. 452–467.

845
Breen, Myles P.; Powell, Jon T.
An investigation into children's perception of the attractiveness and credibility of TV commercials. Paper presented at the Annual Meeting of the Association for Educational Communications and Technology, Philadelphia, Pa., March 22–26, 1971.
n. p.: n. pr. 1971. 8 pp.
(Arlington, Va.: ERIC ED 048 732)

846
Breen, Myles P.; Powell, Jon T.
The relation between attractiveness and credibility of television commercials as perceived by children. A replication. Paper presented at the Annual Meeting of the Central States Speech Association, Minneapolis, April 1973.
n. p.: n. pr. 1973. 15 pp.
(Arlington, Va.: ERIC ED 075 862)

847
Breen, Myles P.; Powell, Jon T.
The relationship between attractiveness and credibility of television commercials as perceived by children.
In: Central States Speech Journal, 24/1973/2, pp. 97–101.

848
Burr, Pat; Burr, Richard M.
Product recognition and premium appeal. How TV sells children.
In: Journal of Communication, 27/1977/1, pp. 115–117.

849
Calder, Bobby J.; Robertson, Thomas S.; Rossiter, John R.
Children's consumer information processing.
In: Communication Research, 2/1975/3, pp. 307–316.

850
Caron, Andre; Ward, Scott
Gift decisions by kids and parents.
In: Journal of Advertising Research, 15/1975/–, pp. 15–20.

851
Children's information processing of television commercial messages.
Appendix III. Paper presented at the Annual Convention of the American
Psychological Association, 81st, Montreal, Canada, August 1973.
Wackman, Daniel B. (Coll.); Ward, Scott (Coll.); Wartella, Ellen (Coll.);
Ettema, James (Coll.)
Cambridge, Mass.: Marketing Science Institute 1973. 41 pp., 26 pp. n. pag.
(Arlington, Va.: ERIC ED 093 465)

852
Clancy-Hepburn, Katherine; Hickey, Anthony A.; Nevill, Gayle
Children's behavior responses to TV food advertisements.
In: Journal of Nutrition Education, 6/1974/3, pp. 93–96.

853
Effects of television advertising on children.
3. Exploring the relationship between television viewing and language
development.
Milkovich, Mark (Coll.); Miller, Mark (Coll.); Bettinghaus, Erwin (Coll.);
Atkin, Charles K. (Coll.)
East Lansing, Mich.: State Univ., College of Communication Arts 1975. 36 pp.
(Arlington, Va.: ERIC ED 116 785)

854
Effects of television commercial disclaimers on the product expectation of
children. How TV sells children.
Liebert, Diane E. (Coll.); Sprafkin, Joyce N. (Coll.); Liebert, Robert M. (Coll.);
Rubinstein, Eli A. (Coll.)
In: Journal of Communication, 27/1977/1, pp. 118–124.

855
Feldman, Shel; Wolf, Abraham; Warmouth, Doris
Parental concern about child-directed commercials. How TV sells children.
In: Journal of Communication, 27/1977/1, pp. 125–137.

856
Frideres, James S.
Advertising, buying patterns and children.
In: Journal of Advertising Research, 13/1973/–, pp. 34–36.

857
Galst, Joann Paley; White, Mary Alice
The unhealthy persuader. The reinforcement value of television and children's
purchase-influencing attempts at the supermarket.
In: Child Development, 47/1976/4, pp. 1089–1096.

858
Goldberg, Marvin E.; Gorn, Gerald J.
Children's reactions to television advertising. An experimental approach.
In: Journal of Consumer Research, 1/1974/September, pp. 69–75.

859
Gorn, Gerald J.; Goldberg, Marvin E.
Children's reactions to television advertising for toys.
n. p.: n. pr. 1974. 24 pp.
(Arlington, Va.: ERIC ED 119 817)

860
Haefner, James E.; Leckenby, John D.; Goldman, Steven L.
The measurement of advertising impact on children. Paper presented at the Annual
Meeting of the American Psychological Association, 83rd, Chicago, Ill., August 30
– Sept. 3, 1975.
n. p.: n. pr. 1975. 30 pp.
(Arlington, Va.: ERIC ED 119 813)

861
Hendon, Donald W.; Duncan, Frances M.; Hendon, Brenda L.
Learning of information in television commercials by gifted, normal and EMR
children. Paper presented at the Annual Meeting of the American Psychological
Association, 82nd, New Orleans, Louis., August 30–Sept. 3, 1974.
n. p.: n. pr. 1974. 20 pp.
(Arlington, Va.: ERIC ED 100 519)

862
Lewis, Charles E.; Lewis, Mary Ann
The impact of television commercials on health-related beliefs and behaviors of children.
In: Pediatrics, 53/1974/3, pp. 431–435.

863
McCullough, J. Lee; Ostrom, Thomas M.
Repetition of highly similar messages and attitude change.
In: Journal of Applied Psychology, 59/1974/3, pp. 395–397.

864
McEwen, William J.; Wittbold, George H.
Assessing the persuasiveness of drug abuse information. Drug abuse information research project.
n. p.: n. pr. 1972. 11 pp.
(Arlington, Va.: ERIC ED 082 266)

865
McEwen, William J.; Wittbold, George H.
Dimensions of response to public service drug abuse information. Drug abuse information project.
n. p.: n. pr. 1972. 19 pp, 2 pp. n. pag.
(Arlington, Va.: ERIC ED 082 256)

866
Milavsky, J. Ronald; Pekowsky, Berton; Stipp, Horst
TV drug advertising and proprietary and illicit drug abuse among teenage boys.
In: Public Opinion Quarterly, 39/1975–76/4, pp. 457–481.

867
Moore, Roy L.; Stephens, Lowndes F.; Moschis, George P.
Mass media and interpersonal influence in adolescent consumer sozialisation.
Paper presented to Mass Communication Division, International
Communication Association, Portland, Oregon, April 14–17, 1976.
n. p.: n. pr. 1976. 20 S.
(Arlington, Va.: ERIC ED 120 881)

868
Moore, Roy L.; Stephens, Lowndes F.
Some communication and demographic determinants of adolescent consumer

learning. Paper presented at the Annual Meeting of the Int. Communication Association, New Orleans, Louisiana, April 17–20, 1974.
n.p.: n. pr. 1974. 24 pp., 9 pp. n. pag.
(Arlington, Va.: ERIC ED 099 901)

869
O'Keefe, M. Timothy
The anti-smoking commercials. A study of television's impact on behavior.
In: Public Opinion Quarterly, 35/1971/–, pp. 242–248.

870
Pierce, Frank N.; Hooper, Leonard J.; Culley, James D.
Perceptions of television advertising directed at children. An investigation of the views of an entire community. April and May, 1974. Paper presented at the Annual Meeting of the Association for Education in Journalism, 57th, San Diego, Ca., August 18–21, 1974.
n. p.: n. pr. 1975. 42 pp.
(Arlington, Va.: ERIC ED 095 559)

871
Prasad, V. Kanti; Rao, Taaniru R.; Sheikh, Anees A.
Mothers vs. commercials. Can people affect television?
In: Journal of Communication, 28/1978/1, pp. 91–96.

872
Prince, Paul; Lazarus, Margaret
Junior consumer protection.
In: Educational Broadcasting, 3/1975/1, pp. 13–15, 30.

873
Rao, Taaniru; Prasad, V. Kanti; Sheikh, Anees A.
Television advertising and its effects on children. A pilot study.
Milwaukee, Wisc.: University of Wisconsin, School of Business Administration
n. d. 41 pp.

874
Robertson, Thomas S.; Rossiter, John R.
Children and commercial persuasion. An attribution theory analysis.
In: Journal of Consumer Research, 1/1974/June, pp. 13–20.

875
Robertson, Thomas S.; Rossiter, John R.
Children's responsiveness to commercials. How TV sells children.
In: Journal of Communication, 27/1977/1, S. 101–106.

876
Robertson, Thomas S.; Rossiter, John R.
Maturational and social factors in children's understanding of TV commercials.
Paper presented at the Annual Meeting of the American Psychological
Association, 83rd, Chicago, Ill., Aug. 30–Sept. 3, 1975.
n. p.: n. pr. 1975. 13 pp.
(Arlington, Va.: ERIC ED 120 758)

877
Robertson, Thomas S.; Rossiter, John R.
Short-run advertising effects on children. A field study.
In: Journal of Marketing Research, 13/1976/–, pp. 68–70.

878
Rossiter, John R.; Robertson, Thomas S.
Canonical analysis of developmental, social, and experimental factors in
children's comprehension of television advertising.
In: Journal of Genetic Psychology, 129/1976/2, pp. 317–327.

879
Rossiter, John R.; Robertson, Thomas S.
Children's TV commercials: Testing the defenses.
In: Journal of Communication, 24/1974/4, pp. 137–144.

880
Rust, Langbourne W.; Watkins, Thomas A.
Children's commercials: Creative Development.
In: Journal of Advertising Research, 15/1975/5, pp. 21–26.

881
Sheikh, Anees A.; Moleski, L. Martin
Children's perception of the value of an advertised product.
In: Journal of Broadcasting, 21/1977/3, pp. 347–354.

882
Sheikh, Anees A.; Moleski, L. Martin
Conflict in the family over commercials. How TV sells children.
In: Journal of Communication, 27/1977/1, pp. 152–157.

883
Stephens, Lowndes F.; Moore, Roy L.
Price accuracy as a consumer skill.
In: Journal of Advertising Research, 15/1975/4, pp. 27–33.

884
Wackman, Daniel B.; Wartella, Ellen; Ward, Scott
Learning to be consumers: The role of the family. How TV sells children.
In: Journal of Communication, 27/1977/1, pp. 138–151.

885
Wackman, Daniel B.; Reale, Greg; Ward, Scott
Racial differences in responses to advertising among adolescents.
In: Television and social behavior. Reports and papers.
    Vol. IV: Television in day-to-day life. Patterns of use.
    Rubinstein, Eli A. (Ed.) et al.
    Washington, D. C.: U. S. Government Printing Office 1972, pp. 543–553.

886
Ward, Scott; Robertson, Thomas S.
Adolescent attitudes toward television advertising. Preliminary findings.
In: Television and social behavior. Reports and papers.
    Vol. IV: Television in day-to-day life. Patterns of use.
    Rubinstein, Eli A. (Ed.) et al.
    Washington, D. C.: U. S. Government Printing Office 1972, pp. 526–542.

887
Ward, Scott; Levinson, David; Wackman, Daniel B.
Children's attention to television advertising.
In: Television and social behavior. Reports and papers.
    Vol. IV: Television in day-to-day life. Patterns of use.
    Rubinstein, Eli A. (Ed.) et al.
    Washington, D. C.: U. S. Government Printing Office 1972, pp. 491–515.

888
Ward, Scott; Wackman, Daniel B.
Children's information processing of television advertising.
In: New models for mass communication research.
Clarke, Peter (Ed.)
Beverly Hills, Ca.: Sage 1973, pp. 119–145.

889
Ward, Scott; Reale, Greg; Levinson, David
Children's perceptions, explanations, and judgements of television advertising.
A further exploration.
In: Television and social behavior. Reports and papers.
Vol. IV: Television in day-to-day life. Patterns of use.
Rubinstein, Eli A. (Ed.) et al.
Washington, D. C.: U. S. Government Printing Office 1972, pp. 468–490.

890
Ward, Scott
Children's reactions to commercials.
In: Journal of Advertising Research, 12/1972/2, pp. 37–45.

891
Ward, Scott; Wackman, Daniel B.
Family and media influence on adolescent consumer learning.
In: Television and social behavior. Reports and papers.
Vol. IV: Television in day-to-day life. Patterns of use.
Rubinstein, Eli A. (Ed.) et al.
Washington, D. C.: U. S. Government Printing Office 1972, pp. 554–567.
Also in:
Mass communications and youth. Some current perspectives.
Kline, Gerald F. (Ed.) et al.
Beverly Hills, Ca.: Sage 1971, pp. 113–125.
Also in:
American Behavioral Scientist, 14/1971/3, pp. 415–427.

892
Ward, Scott; Wackman, Daniel B.
Television advertising and intrafamily influence. Children's purchase influence attempts and parental yielding.
In: Television and social behavior. Reports and papers.
Vol. IV: Television in day-to-day life. Patterns of use.
Rubinstein, Eli A. (Ed.) et al.
Washington, D. C.: U. S. Government Printing Office 1972, pp. 516–525.

893
Wartella, Ellen; Ettema, James S.
A cognitive developmental study of children's attention to television commercials.
In: Communication Research, 1/1974/1, S. 69–88.

894
Wartella, Ellen; Ettema, James S.
The role of stimulus complexity in children's attention to television commercials. A developmental study.
n. p.: n. pr. 1973. 18 pp. Appendix.
(Arlington, Va.: ERIC ED 084 537)

895
Williams, Sally
Television and the young consumer. An analysis of consumer needs of children and a proposal for the utilization of television to meet these needs.
Committee on Children's Television, San Francisco, Ca. (Ed.)
n. p.: n. pr. 1974. 33 pp.
(Arlington, Va.: ERIC ED 089 738)

896
Wittmann, Ilse
Kind und Werbefernsehen. Eine Untersuchung mit 12jährigen.
(Children and television commercials. A study of 12 year old children.)
München: n. pr. 1971. 72 pp., 40 pp. Appx.

12. RESEARCH AGENDA AND RECOMMENDATIONS

897
Anderson, Kristin; Comstock, George; Dennis, Nancy
Recommendations for priorities. Research on television and the young.
In: Journal of Communication, 26/1976/2, pp. 98–107.
German translation:
Anderson, Kristin; Comstock, George; Dennis, Nancy
Forschungen zum Thema Kind und Fernsehen – Empfehlungen für Forschungs-
prioritäten.
In: Fernsehen und Bildung, 10/1976/1–2, pp. 123–133.

898
Berry, Gordon L.
Research, television and the child. The need for risk-takers.
Paper presented at the Biennial Meeting of the Society for Research in Child
Development, Denver, Col., April 11, 1975.
n. p.: n. pr. 1975. 8 pp.
(Arlington, Va.: ERIC ED 111 505)

899
Clarke, Peter; Kline, Gerald F.
Media effects reconsidered. Some new strategies for communication research.
In: Communication Research, 1/1974/2, pp. 224–240.

German translation:
Clarke, Peter; Kline, F. Gerald
Medienwirkungen neu überdacht. Einige neue Strategien zur Kommunikations-
forschung.
In: Rundfunk und Fernsehen, 22/1974/1, pp. 37–52.

900
Clarke, Peter
Some proposals for continuing research on youth and the mass media.
In: Mass communications and youth. Some current perspectives.
    Kline, Gerald F. (Ed.) et al.
    Beverly Hills, Ca.: Sage 1971, pp. 11–20.

901
Comstock, George
Priorities for action-oriented psychological studies of television and behavior.

Prepared for the symposium 'Television effects. Research needs from an action perspective' at the Annual Meeting of the American Psychological Association, San Francisco, Calif., August 26–30, 1977.
Rand Corporation (Ed.)
Santa Monica, Calif.: Rand Corporation 1977. 14 S.

902
Comstock, George
Research and the constructive aspects of television in children's lives. A forecast.
Paper delivered at the symposium 'Perspectives on the Influence of Television on the Development of Children' at the Annual Meeting of the American Educational Research Association, San Francisco, California, April 19–23, 1976.
Santa Monica, Ca.: Rand 1976. 18 pp.
(Arlington, Va.: ERIC ED 122 857)

903
Comstock, George; Lindsey, Georg
Television and human behavior. The research horizon, future and present.
Fisher, Marylin (Coll.)
Santa Monica, Ca.: Rand 1975. 120 pp.

904
Comstock, George
Television and the young. Setting the stage for a research agenda.
Paper presented at the conference 'Research on television and children and youth. What are the priorities?', Reston, Va.: Nov. 5–7, 1975.
Santa Monica, Ca.: Rand 1975. 18 pp.
(Arlington, Va.: ERIC ED 121 325)

905
Fowles, Barbara R.; Horner, Vivian M.
A suggested research strategy. The effects of television on children and adolescents.
In: Journal of Communication, 25/1975/4, pp. 98–101.

906
Graves, Sherryl Browne
Television's impact on children. Roles for research and policy.
Paper presented at the Annual Meeting of the Telecommunications Policy Research Conference, Airlie, Va., April 23, 1976.
n. p.: n. pr. 1976. 14 pp.
(Arlington, Va.: ERIC ED 125 597)

907
Katz, Elihu
Social research on broadcasting. Proposals for further development. A report to
the British Broadcasting Corporation.
London: BBC 1977. 116 pp.

908
Leifer, Aimée Dorr; Gordon, Neal J.; Graves, Sherryl Browne
Children and television. Recommended directions for future efforts. Final report to
the Office of Child Development, Department of Health, Education and Welfare.
Cambridge, Mass.: Harvard University, Center for Research in Children's
Television 1973, 23 pp.

German translation of abridged version:
Leifer, Aimée Dorr; Gordon, Neal J.; Graves, Sherryl Browne
Kind und Fernsehen. Aktionsplan für künftige Forschungen.
In: Fernsehen und Bildung, 9/1975/1, pp. 9–28.

909
Mielke, Keith W.; Bryant, Jennings, Jr.
Formative research in attention and appeal. A series of proposals.
New York, N. Y.: Children's Television Workshop 1972. 21 pp.
(Arlington, Va.: ERIC ED 126 867)

910
Mielke, Keith W.; Bryant, Jennings, Jr.
Formative research in comprehension of CTW programs. A series of proposals.
New York, N. Y.: Children's Television Workshop 1972. 13 pp.
(Arlington, Va.: ERIC ED 126 868)

911
Report of research workshop on television and social behavior, Washington,
D. C., May 31–June 1, 1972.
Bethesda, Md.: National Institute of Mental Health 1974. 13 pp.
(Arlington, Va.: ERIC ED 087 379)

912
Schleicher, Klaus
The use of television in pre-school education in sparsely populated areas.
Strasbourg: Council for Cultural Co-operation, Committee for General and
Technical Education 1977. 47 pp.

913
Sturm, Hertha
Vorschläge zur Abschätzung von Fernsehwirkungen auf Kinder.
(Proposals for the appraisal of television effects on children.)
In: Fernseh-Kritik. Kinder vor dem Bildschirm.
    Heygster, Anna-Luise (Ed.) et al.
    Mainz: v. Hase und Köhler 1974, pp. 29–47.

914
Television and children. Priorities for research. Report of a conference at
Reston, Virginia, Nov. 5–7, 1975.
Ford Foundation, New York (Ed.)
New York, N. Y.: Ford Foundation, Office of Reports n. d. (probably 1976).
38 pp.
(Arlington, Va.: ERIC ED 125 574)

AUTHOR INDEX

Parton, David A. 272, 597
Patrick, Helen 227
Paulson, F. Leon 729, 739
Pekowsky, Berton 552, 866
Pena, Deagelia 795, 803
Perry, David G. 357
Perry, Louise C. 357
Pflüger, Ulrike 813
Phelps, Erin M. 266
Pick, A. D. 697
Pierce, Frank N. 870
Pietilä, Veikko 67
Pingree, Suzanne 375, 381
Pisarek, Walery 19
Plost, Myrna 358
Polsky, Richard M. 740
Polsky, Samuel 573, 574
Pool, Ithiel de Sola 45, 134
Popitz, Heinrich 503
Poulos, Rita W. 129, 130, 509, 670, 680, 683, 684
Powell, Jon T. 845, 846, 847
Powell, R. J. 203
Prasad, V. Kanti 443, 831, 871, 873
Prawat, Dorothy M. 181
Prawat, Richard S. 181
Prince, Paul 872
Prokop, Dieter 63, 64, 471
Pross, Harry 70
Pusser, H. Ellison 705

Quanty, M. B. 644
Quarles, R. C. 7

Rabinovitch, Martin S. 606, 628
Radio and Television Culture Research Institute, Tokyo 149
Rand Corporation, Santa Monica, Ca. 818
Rao, Taaniru R. 831, 871, 873
Rapoport, Max 188
Rarick, David L. 556
Ray, Michael L. 328
Reale, Greg 885, 889
Reeves, Barbara Frengel 745, 746
Reeves, Byron 161, 267, 268, 269, 292, 293, 354
Reid, George R. 298

Renckstorf, Karsten 71, 72, 747
Rennie, David L. 291
Reyes-Lagunes, Isabel 741
Richards, W. D. 7
Ridberg, Eugene H. 300
Riegel, Klaus F. 127, 301
Rivers, William L. 21
Roberts, Donald F. 69, 133, 134, 375, 381, 576, 810
Robertson, Thomas S. 346, 830, 849, 874, 875, 876, 877, 878, 879, 886
Robinson, John P. 73, 558
Roden, Aubrey H. 619
Rogers, Janet M. 752
Rogers, Ronald W. 629
Ronneberger, Franz 79, 142
Rop, Ilse 598
Rosen, Marvin J. 358
Rosenbaum, Leonard L. 322
Rosenbaum, William B. 322
Rosengren, Karl Erik 74, 210
Ross, James 187
Ross, Lee B. 599
Rossiter, John R. 346, 849, 874, 875, 876, 877, 878, 879
Rubin, Alan M. 165, 382
Rubin, Donald B. 777, 778, 790
Rubinstein, Eli A. 58, 73, 162, 179, 191, 202, 212, 404, 510, 512, 513, 514, 515, 516, 524, 525, 670, 683, 844, 854, 885, 886, 887, 889, 891, 892
Rust, Holger 243
Rust, Langbourne W. 791, 792, 793, 880
Rutt, Theodor 226
Rydin, Ingegerd 182, 279, 280

Salomon, Gavriel 301, 302, 712, 753, 754, 755, 756
Samuels, Bruce 757
Savitsky, Jeffrey C. 629
Saxer, Ulrich 135
Schäfer, Harald 347
Scharff, William H. 661
Schenk, Michael 76
Scherer, Klaus R. 323
Schleicher, Klaus 758, 912
Schlottmann, Robert S. 661

161

Swift, Betty 229, 230
Swinford, Helen Lee 204
Sylves, David 767

Tada, T. 149
Taipale, Hannu 295
Takeshima, Y. 149
Talbott, Albert D. 606
Tannenbaum, Percy H. 510, 659
Tausch, Anne-Marie 603
Taylor, Lorne J. 768
Taylor, Peter H. 256
Teasdale, G. R. 723
Teevan, James T. Jr. 549, 560
Teichert, Will 81, 82, 83
Television Research Committee, London 194
Thelen, Mark H. 283, 284, 291, 304, 319, 326, 611
Thomas, Margaret H. 587, 608, 609, 610
Thomas, Sally A. 582, 630
Thornton, J. E. 228
Tichenor, Phillip J. 31
Tims, Albert R. 216
Tipton, Leonard P. 369
Tolley, Howard Jr. 383
Toomey, Tim C. 327
Torney, Judith V. 826
Townsend, J. E. 556
Tuchman, Sam 552
Tunstall, Jeremy 65, 194
Turk, Lorraine 730
Turner, Charles W. 660

Ubbens, Wilbert 16, 25, 26
Ulrich, Rober E. 769
United States Department of Health, Education, and Welfare 24, 511, 512, 513, 514, 515, 516, 703

Valenzuela, Nicholas A. 809
Verlag Volker Spiess, Berlin 16
Verna, Mary Ellen 13
Vitouch, Peter 643
Vlahos, Mantha 191
Vogg, Günther 176
Vondracek, Fred 600
Vonhoff, Renate 317

Vowinckel, Gerhard 770, 771

Wackman, Daniel B. 144, 368, 833, 835, 851, 884, 885, 887, 888, 891, 892
Wade, Serena 247, 248
Walbeck, Nancy H. 671
Walder, Leopold O. 530, 531, 537, 540, 543, 555, 557, 561
Walters, Richard H. 468
Ward, Eric F. 794
Ward, Marilyn D. 794
Ward, Scott 328, 369, 832, 833, 834, 835, 844, 850, 851, 884, 885, 886, 887, 888, 889, 890, 891, 892
Warmouth, Doris 855
Wart, Geraldine van 806, 807
Wartella, Ellen 144, 835, 851, 884, 893, 894
Watkins, Thomas A. 880
Watt, James H. 563
Weigel, Russell H. 329
Weiss, Walter 86
Weissenborn, Rainer 33
Wells, Alan 62
Welzel, Susanne 27
Werner, Anita 170
Werner, Peter 140, 825
West, Gerald T. 377
Westby, Sally Driscoll 252, 564
Wetstone, Harriet S. 823
White, Mary Alice 857
Wigand, Rolf T. 819, 820, 821
Wilde, Robert J. 186
Wilder, Gita Jane 772
Wilkins, Judy L. 661
Will, Edward E. 687
Williams, Frederick 209, 807, 808, 809
Williams, Sally 895
Williams, Wenmouth Jr. 662
Wilson, Edward C. 330
Windahl, Swen 74, 75, 210
Wingert, Gerhard 813
Wissenschaftliches Institut für Jugend- und Bildungsfragen in Film und Fernsehen, München 27, 813
Wittbold, George H. 864, 865
Wittmann, Ilse 896

SUBJECT INDEX

marital roles 349, 350
maturity 149, 876
mass communication research 28–87
mass media functions 105, 146, 147, 148, 149, 155, 157, 158, 161, 162, 186, 199–201, 220–222, 223, 244, 245
mass media use 145, 146, 149, 150, 152, 155, 157, 159, 162, 165, 166, 168, 174, 175, 179, 180, 184, 185, 186, 193, 197, 199–201, 217, 220–222, 223, 224–226, 229, 230, 231, 233–235, 238, 242, 244, 246–249, 363, 365–367, 370, 372, 375, 379–381, 535, 541, 867, 868, 891
media education 89–91, 104, 120, 126, 204, 258, 259, 264, 265
media preferences 159, 189, 190, 230, 376, 822
media-specific effects 140–142, 296, 299, 330
mentally retarded children 94, 207, 208, 285, 286, 324, 861
Mexico 548, 711, 741
'Mister Roger's Neighborhood' 281, 282, 589, 600, 672–675, 681, 685, 705
moral development 287
moral judgement 287, 297, 311, 635, 636
mothers' attitudes 174, 179, 180, 184, 191, 526, 748–750, 815, 841, 848, 871
motivation of actions 564–568, 576
motives for viewing 155, 157, 158, 165, 168, 192, 235, 238, 241, 535, 538
music 309

Netherlands 719
neuroticism 213
news exposure 815, 818
news media 242, 363, 370, 373, 374, 377, 496, 815, 822
newspaper reading 168, 192, 246, 368, 373, 374, 380
non-verbal responses 181, 309, 766
Norway 1, 2, 15, 20, 110, 170, 317
nutrition education 895

observational learning 128, 129, 138, 255, 256, 272, 289, 290, 300, 304, 357, 597, 682, 842

occupational aspirations 170, 233, 234, 352, 358
occupational roles 352, 354, 358
opinion formation 249, 369
opinion leadership 185

para-social interaction 210
parent – child relationship 107, 120, 126, 162, 163, 167, 188, 191, 215, 240, 259, 265, 274, 281, 286, 292, 328, 332, 345, 526, 528, 550, 551, 655, 714, 720, 730, 755, 850, 860, 878, 882
parent participation 714, 720, 755, 795
parental control 103, 126, 148, 149, 160, 162, 163, 166, 167, 168, 174, 176, 179, 180, 184, 188, 191, 196, 203, 204, 206, 215–217, 240, 332, 336, 337, 528, 855
parental viewing time 215, 216, 217
parental yielding 841, 848, 856, 892
party identification 370, 375
passivity 202, 214
peer group orientation 348
peer models 355, 583, 590, 594, 632, 682
peer relationship 120, 162, 166, 196, 203, 216, 234, 237, 292, 348, 540, 587, 655, 673, 867, 875
perception 182, 251, 313, 314, 327, 345
perception of TV commercials 845–847, 870, 872, 874, 881, 889
perceptional development 263, 787
peripheral content 254, 262, 279, 280, 575
person perception 162, 267, 268, 269, 271, 285, 293, 312, 320, 349, 534, 544
personality development 129
personality factors 194, 198, 203, 213, 227, 228, 282, 573, 574, 657, 660
persuasion 310
persuasiveness 864, 865
Piagetian theory 140, 142, 144, 182, 287, 579–581, 588, 591–594, 598, 599, 601, 619, 626, 627, 632, 876, 878
play behavior 105, 162, 171, 175, 177, 179, 180, 202, 228, 281, 282, 305, 689, 691, 802, 813, 836, 837
Poland 19, 294
political attitudes 364–367, 370, 371, 373–375, 377, 380, 382, 383, 826

Internationales Zentralinstitut für
das Jugend- und Bildungsfernsehen
(IZI)

Communication Research
and Broadcasting

No. 1

School Radio in Europe
A documentation
with contributions given at the
European School Radio Conference,
Munich 1977
1979. 198 p. DM 28.—.
ISBN 3-598-20200-8

No. 2

Effects and Functions
of Television:
Children and Adolescents
A bibliography of selected research
literature 1970—1978
Compiled by
Manfred Meyer and Ursula Nissen
1979. 172 p. DM 28.—.
ISBN 3-598-20201-6

No. 3

Women, Communication,
and Careers
Edited by
Marianne Grewe-Partsch und
Gertrude J. Robinson
1980. 138 p. DM 28.—.
ISBN 3-598-20202-4

Fernsehen und Bildung
Internationale Zeitschrift für
Medienpsychologie und
Medienpraxis

Special English Issues

Television and Socialization
Processes in the Family
A documentation of the
Prix Jeunesse Seminar 1975
1976. 192 p. DM 24.—
ISBN 3-7940-3368-X

Perception – Development –
Communication
1978. 118 p. DM 24.—
ISBN 3-7940-3367-1

K·G·Saur München · New York · London · Paris

K·G·Saur Verlag KG · Postfach 711009 · 8000 Munchen 71 · Tel. (089) 798901
K·G·Saur Publishing, Inc. · 1995 Broadway · New York, N.Y. 10023 · Tel. 212 873-2100
K·G·Saur Ltd. · 1-19 New Oxford Street · London WC1A 1NE · Tel. 01-404-4818;
K·G·Saur Editeur S.A.R.L. · 38, rue de Bassano · 75008 Paris · Téléphone 723 55-10